The History of Political Thought: A Very Short Introduction

VERY SHORT INTRODUCTIONS are for anyone wanting a stimulating and accessible way into a new subject. They are written by experts, and have been translated into more than 45 different languages.

The series began in 1995, and now covers a wide variety of topics in every discipline. The VSI library currently contains over 700 volumes—a Very Short Introduction to everything from Psychology and Philosophy of Science to American History and Relativity—and continues to grow in every subject area.

Very Short Introductions available now:

ABOLITIONISM Richard S. Newman
THE ABRAHAMIC RELIGIONS
    Charles L. Cohen
ACCOUNTING Christopher Nobes
ADOLESCENCE Peter K. Smith
ADVERTISING Winston Fletcher
AERIAL WARFARE Frank Ledwidge
AESTHETICS Bence Nanay
AFRICAN AMERICAN RELIGION
    Eddie S. Glaude Jr
AFRICAN HISTORY John Parker and
    Richard Rathbone
AFRICAN POLITICS Ian Taylor
AFRICAN RELIGIONS
    Jacob K. Olupona
AGEING Nancy A. Pachana
AGNOSTICISM Robin Le Poidevin
AGRICULTURE Paul Brassley and
    Richard Soffe
ALEXANDER THE GREAT
    Hugh Bowden
ALGEBRA Peter M. Higgins
AMERICAN BUSINESS HISTORY
    Walter A. Friedman
AMERICAN CULTURAL
    HISTORY Eric Avila
AMERICAN FOREIGN RELATIONS
    Andrew Preston
AMERICAN HISTORY Paul S. Boyer
AMERICAN IMMIGRATION
    David A. Gerber
AMERICAN INTELLECTUAL
    HISTORY
    Jennifer Ratner-Rosenhagen

AMERICAN LEGAL HISTORY
    G. Edward White
AMERICAN MILITARY HISTORY
    Joseph T. Glatthaar
AMERICAN NAVAL HISTORY
    Craig L. Symonds
AMERICAN POETRY David Caplan
AMERICAN POLITICAL HISTORY
    Donald Critchlow
AMERICAN POLITICAL PARTIES
    AND ELECTIONS L. Sandy Maisel
AMERICAN POLITICS
    Richard M. Valelly
THE AMERICAN PRESIDENCY
    Charles O. Jones
THE AMERICAN REVOLUTION
    Robert J. Allison
AMERICAN SLAVERY
    Heather Andrea Williams
THE AMERICAN SOUTH
    Charles Reagan Wilson
THE AMERICAN WEST Stephen Aron
AMERICAN WOMEN'S HISTORY
    Susan Ware
AMPHIBIANS T. S. Kemp
ANAESTHESIA Aidan O'Donnell
ANALYTIC PHILOSOPHY
    Michael Beaney
ANARCHISM Colin Ward
ANCIENT ASSYRIA Karen Radner
ANCIENT EGYPT Ian Shaw
ANCIENT EGYPTIAN ART AND
    ARCHITECTURE Christina Riggs
ANCIENT GREECE Paul Cartledge

Available soon:

For more information visit our website

www.oup.com/vsi/

Richard Whatmore

THE HISTORY
OF POLITICAL
THOUGHT

A Very Short Introduction

OXFORD
UNIVERSITY PRESS

Great Clarendon Street, Oxford, OX2 6DP,
United Kingdom

Oxford University Press is a department of the University of Oxford.
It furthers the University's objective of excellence in research, scholarship,
and education by publishing worldwide. Oxford is a registered trade mark of
Oxford University Press in the UK and in certain other countries

First Edition published in 2021

Impression: 2

Published in the United States of America by Oxford University Press
198 Madison Avenue, New York, NY 10016, United States of America

British Library Cataloguing in Publication Data
Data available

Library of Congress Control Number: 2021942157

ISBN 978-0-19-885372-5

Printed in Great Britain by
Ashford Colour Press Ltd, Gosport, Hampshire

For Knud Haakonssen

Contents

Acknowledgements

This book is dedicated to my close friend Knud Haakonssen, a master scholar and one of the best and most generous historians of political thought. Special thanks go to Christopher de Bellaigue, Tony Black, Michael Drolet, James Harris, Béla Kapossy, Konrad Lawson, Gabriel Sabbagh, Max Skjönsberg, Michael Sonenscher, Koen Stapelbroek, Keith Tribe, Xilu Wang, Lina Weber, and anonymous referees. Jess Whatmore acted as research assistant and I'm grateful for his wide-ranging expertise. It was a pleasure working with Jenny Nugee, Luciana O'Flaherty, and OUP more generally. As always my greatest debt is to my wife Ruth Woodfield and our sons Jess, Kim, and Davy Whatmore.

List of illustrations

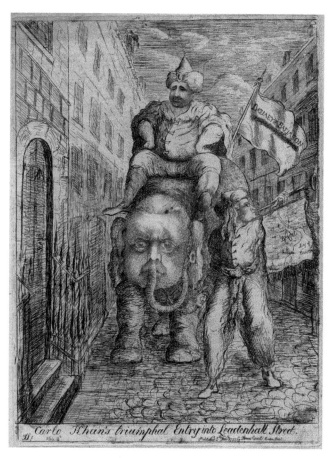

Carlo Khan's triumphal Entry into Leadenhall Street.

1. James Sayers, *Carlo Khan's Triumphal Entry into Leadenhall Street* (5 December 1783).

Chapter 1
History and politics

Hats and elephants

What is the corpulent man doing riding the elephant with a
human face (Figure 1)? Why is he dressed like a pasha and what is
the meaning of the banner held by the thinner bespectacled man
beside him? Why are they walking down Leadenhall Street? What
is the meaning of the image? The history of political thought can
answer such questions. The obese figure is Charles James Fox, an
English Whig politician famous for his debauched life and
gambling addiction. He is riding an elephant with the face of the
prime minister Lord North, infamous for continuing the war
against the thirteen colonies that became the United States of
America. The man leading the elephant is Edmund Burke, still
described by many as the founder of modern conservative
doctrine. At the time, Fox and Burke were pushing through the
British parliament a bill to reduce the power of the East India
Company. Burke especially was critical of the horrors practised
by empire builders, epitomized for him by the British
governor-general of Bengal, Warren Hastings. Burke was soon to
spend years seeking to impeach Hastings for corruption.

The print by James Sayers of December 1783 does not applaud the
actions of Fox and Burke in promoting decolonization in India as
well as in North America. Rather, Sayers accuses both men of

seeking to turn themselves into what was called at the time 'oriental despots', introducing into Britain foreign tyranny and an addiction to luxury associated with the East. This is why the flag has Fox's traditional self-depiction of 'man of the people' scribbled over and replaced by 'ΒΑΣΙVEVS ΒΑΣΙΛΕΩΝ' or 'king of kings'. Burke's map of India has territories from Delhi to Fort St George and the Bay of Bengal specified as being for 'C-F' or Charles Fox's personal empire. Their takeover is to be presented to the offices of the East India Company in Leadenhall Street in the City of London. Impending disaster is signalled by the raven above with an etching 'The night Crow cried foreboding luckless Time'. This is a reference to Shakespeare's play *Henry VI, Part Three* (Act 5, Scene 6) where the king curses Richard III (Gloucester) for his evil deeds before being murdered by him. The print was so successful in maligning Fox's and Burke's India Bill that it was rejected by parliament. North's government soon fell. Sayers's warning was that those who portray themselves as the friends of the people can easily be tempted into tyranny. The image epitomizes commonplace perceptions of the East, contributing to the positive 'othering of Europe' and the prejudice of orientalism.

History explains politics. The history of political thought reveals the variety of perceptions of political projects, actions, and utterances, the hopes of their perpetrators and the fears of their critics. Knowledge of the history of ideologies can be revelatory. It makes us aware that those who wear Pussyhats (Figure 2) today are not only ridiculing Donald Trump and providing an alternative to his Make America Great Again caps but are also affirming a long tradition of liberty headgear going back to the Roman *pileus* or hat worn by emancipated slaves. Yet Pussyhats resemble Phrygian caps symbolic of liberty (Figure 3). Phrygia was a Bronze Age kingdom in Anatolia. King Midas of Phrygia, renowned for his lust for gold, can be seen on ancient Greek coins wearing such a cap, as can the Trojan hero Paris in Roman art because Troy too was in the Roman province of Hellespontine Phrygia. Phrygian caps, like Fox's turban, have orientalist origins

2. Pussyhat.

in their association of the East with luxury, empire, and the mysticism of the religious Mithras cult. How they became across Europe the bright red Phrygian caps symbolic of a willingness to die in the cause of freedom is the kind of story the history of political thought can unravel.

Liberty in history

A useful starting point in the history of political thought is to take one of the most inspiring utterances ever made, 'Man is born free but is everywhere in chains.' Taken at face value, Jean-Jacques Rousseau's infamous commencement of his *Contrat social* (1762) was a call to rebellion and acknowledgement of ubiquitous human bondage. This was one reason why his book was burned for being destructive of government and religion at Geneva and in France only months after it was published. Rousseau was then attacked for being an incarnation of one of John Milton's hell-bound demons described in *Paradise Lost*. It was also why Rousseau's work was widely celebrated and denounced decades later for

3. Phrygian cap.

inspiring the French Revolution. Rousseau's writings appeared to have a clear message: protest and rebel against the corruption and tyranny you find all around you.

The censors who cast Rousseau's works into the flames may not have read them. Nor may the revolutionaries who venerated Rousseau as the patron saint of rebels. Certainly neither party understood Rousseau's profound political message. Rousseau, in subsequent writing and in numerous letters to friends asserted that his *Contrat social* had been entirely misunderstood. His book had asserted that once liberty was lost it could only with difficulty be recovered. Where corruption reigned—for Rousseau this was epitomized by Paris—there could be no possibility of successful reform let alone popular revolution. Rousseau's broader point was that political argument, especially in democratic fora, was likely to be meaningless because it was so easy to delude the people through rhetoric or their admiration of rich and powerful demagogues. Political thinking was the most difficult of subjects, Rousseau felt, because small states—the only states where people could ever be happy or free—were in the modern world dominated by larger or wealthier states. The latter were addicted to the pursuit of power through money; the lust for gain corrupted everything in commercial societies. The consequence was that reforms, however well intentioned, so often went astray (Figure 4).

Recovering what Rousseau actually thought is one of the goals of the history of political thought. It is worthwhile because individuals such as Rousseau, a watchmaker's son born in the Calvinist republic of Geneva, still have a lot to say to us. In Rousseau's case he saw himself to be sending a warning to people living in commercial societies that they were doomed to repeat a cycle of war and rule by tyrannical Caesar figures. Small states were likely to become endangered species. Politics would increasingly be seen through a glass darkly, especially by credulous populations, and steps needed to be taken to address the deep malaise. Revolution, rather than making things better, would always make things worse.

Surely, it might be said, all that anyone has to do to understand Rousseau is to read his books, either in translation or in the

4. James Gillray, *Siège de la Colonne de Pompée: Science in the Pillory* (6 March 1799). *Note Rousseau's Contrat social.*

original language? One of the points that will be made here is that if you want to recover the historical meaning of an author's argument you have to reconstruct the assumptions about politics in the author's own time. You need to immerse yourself in the writings of the period with the aim of understanding what mattered to political actors, what they perceived themselves to be doing and what their senses were of the range of options open to them. It was inconceivable for Rousseau, for example, to imagine a democracy in a large state. He would have said it could not exist because popular free government relies on people sharing a culture and being willing to sacrifice themselves for one another, something only possible where states are small enough for citizens to know and appreciate one another.

Do such opinions matter? Recasting an author's ideas by reference to contemporary controversy helps to register their ongoing import. Rather than being seen as a proto-democrat or revolutionary it makes more sense to understand Rousseau as those in his own time did, diagnosing contemporary ills in addition to those that were on the horizon. Rousseau questioned whether people who called themselves republicans lived in sustainable republics and whether those who called themselves democrats were in fact making a category mistake. Rousseau was falsely accused by critics of being an enemy of the present, an advocate of life as hunter gatherers or noble savages and of wanting, as his enemy Voltaire once put it, to return humanity to walking on all fours. Rousseau loved plants, animals, and indigenous societies because he considered them to be closer to nature, but he was brutally realistic about politics past and present. Some of his closest readers called him a Cynic, in part because he was so clear-headed about the difficulty of solving problems in human societies without recourse to war.

People gathered together by politics, according to Rousseau, so often became like members of missionary religions, seeking to battle members of other churches in order to convert them. People within churches, however committed they might initially be to their brothers and sisters who shared their beliefs, were likely to split off and form new sects, initially deemed purer than those they were replacing. Impulses to convert and dominate by incorporating others into your own empire had somehow to be avoided. Such an aspiration was difficult enough in a single society. Between competing nations it was next to impossible. One of the points Rousseau made was that real change in politics only occurred after the experience of acute crisis. Once humans relaxed again, when Damocles' sword appeared to have disappeared from the air, the old corruptions would return. Despite the gargantuan difficulties faced by politics proper it was the most essential work in the world, Rousseau said, to defend the small communities in which people lived across the globe as they were the places where people were happier and less disposed to violence. Rousseau considered such communities to be ever more endangered by the progress of commercial societies seeking empire. Although he was open about his own failure to find solutions, admitting that the *Contrat social* was an unfinished book in consequence, being aware of the nature of the crisis and the partial solutions to date that were certain to fail represented a significant contribution to knowledge; limits, uncertainties, unintended consequences, and failures perhaps amounted to political wisdom itself for Rousseau.

Today we live in a period when crisis is once again all around us. The democratic and liberal politics that were for a long time seen to be second nature, even an 'end of history', are now recognized to be fragile. Many commentators argue that liberal democracy may not survive the current generation. In addition, the combinations of politics and commercial society that brought industrial development through the 20th century to so much of the globe, always in the form of the unparalleled exploitation of natural resources but with a Liberal or a Marxist justificatory veneer, can now be seen to be threatening life on earth. When change is necessary, looking to the past becomes vital for the simple reason that past generations have faced comparable predicaments. In politics they have experienced everything, and nothing at all is new. That is why the history of political thought as a subject is more essential than ever before. This book describes the currently dominant approaches to the subject and some of the issues that the history of political thought faces going into the future.

Chapter 2
Definitions and justifications

Varieties of histories of political thought

The history of political thought as a distinctive field of research is a recent development. Historically, however, every society has formulated histories of political thought from the anodyne to the systematic. In the past, where politics has been closely entwined with the worship of deities on whom the survival of a society is held to depend, myths and histories become enmeshed. Using the heralded opinions of the gods to undertake sometimes radical innovation is commonplace in the history of political thought. In order to reduce the power of Egypt's priesthood, Pharaoh Akhenaten declared the sun god to be the only deity and himself to be a descendant. The Roman Emperor Constantine's motto 'by the cross I will conquer', said to have been coined after defeating his rival Maxentius at the Milvian Bridge in 312 CE, was used to justify both the expansion of empire and Christian conversion.

Adhering to the word of God or violating it could mean life, death, or slavery. Islamic traders in the interior of the Swahili coast during the medieval period considered those they enslaved to be infidels and therefore legitimate targets. They transported their human property to Arabia, Egypt, or Iraq. Enacting the apparent will of God could also mean salvation in the next life. Pope Urban II in 1095 declared that it was the duty of all Christians to take Jerusalem from the Muslims and that anyone who took part in what became the First Crusade would see their souls travel directly to heaven, much like certain Islamist understandings of Jihad today. Another example comes from the history of Buddhism. In order to convert the Mongols, the 3rd Dalai Lama Sonam Gyatsho guaranteed in 1578 that his patron Altan Khan was a reincarnation of Kublai Khan and that his next reincarnation would undoubtedly occur in Mongolia, something which occurred with the disputed incarnation of Yonten Gyatso as 4th Dalai Lama, himself a descendent of Altan Khan.

If the present is widely recognized to be a diminished version of the past, then historical politics become reified. Inhabitants of Abyssinia in early modern times lived among giant monoliths built using lost techniques and inscribed with a language the locals did not understand. King Ezana of Aksum in the 4th century CE converted to Christianity but the empire declined over following centuries and ultimately collapsed after defeat in war either by the Jewish queen Yodit (Gudit) in 960 or by a pagan queen Bani al-Hamwiyah of the al-Damutah tribe. The historian Edward Gibbon later wrote that after Ezana's loss Ethiopia slept through a millennium-long dark age. Nevertheless, Ethiopia survived as an independent Christian state despite being surrounded by Islamic polities, as the Prophet Muhammad forbade Jihad after his daughter had been given refuge during the exile from Mecca. Perspectives upon history have always been key to Islamic political thought.

Across Europe and Asia belief in the superiority of ancient Rome to contemporary society was prevalent from medieval times to the 18th century. Roman and Greek culture was not only venerated but inspired a rebirth of learning, now termed the Renaissance. Especially marked in the city states of Italy and spreading through the actions of travelling humanists, the Renaissance saw ancient manuscripts copied and transported westwards, saved from destruction within the Byzantine and Ottoman empires.

Translated into Latin, annotated, and published, these texts had a transformative impact upon life and thought. Classical writing, artefacts, and art conveyed the view to numerous Europeans that their achievements in philosophy, art, literature, and military tactics were inferior to those of the Romans.

Even as the arts, letters, and technology were seen to have improved, a quarrel erupted between those who believed in the superiority of the ancients and those who embraced the achievements of the modern world. On one side of the argument was the French poet Nicolas Boileau, who held that imitation of the ancients was the most apt aspiration for inferiors in the present. On the other, the polymath Bernard le Bovier de Fontenelle hailed the superiority of modern refinement and scientific and technological achievements. The battle was brilliantly lampooned by Jonathan Swift (Figure 5).

A
Full and True Account
OF THE
BATTEL
Fought laſt *FRIDAY*,
Between the
Antient and the *Modern*
BOOKS
IN
St. *JAMES*'s
LIBRARY.

LONDON:
Printed in the Year, MDCCX.

5. Jonathan Swift, frontispiece, *An Account of a Battel between the Ancient and Modern Books* (1704).

If national myths in culture justify combat with other nations or peoples or describe unjustly thwarted destinies in recent or ancient history, these beliefs will be reflected in the history of political thought. If you perceive yourselves to be God's chosen people in a particular nation or tract of land, history can be used to justify acts of violence for the acquisition of additional territory. Although modern Italians are descendants of Lombards, Ostrogoths, Franks, and Normans, among many others, the national myth of being exclusively Roman was used by the fascist dictator Benito Mussolini in the 1930s to justify the invasion of Abyssinia to add to the colonies of Eritrea and Somalia secured during the 19th-century European scramble for Africa. Adolf Hitler called the Treaty of Versailles ending the First World War a monstrous violation of the greatness and rights of the German people. In this view, the Germans had been victors over Rome at the Teutoburg Forest and the iron will of the German people manifested itself in history until they were betrayed by foreign traitors.

In the case of the United Kingdom, a country widely perceived to be in decline since it lost its empire, proposals have been made by governments to instil facts about past victories in war into the heads of primary and secondary school children. In Scotland, a different version of the history of political thought is widely propagated, describing the oppression of native Scots by the English and the loss of liberty, with a view to its recovery through independence. In Russia a powerful role is played by national myths about Eurasianism, the belief that linked nomad tribes from the steppes, including the Scythians, Huns, Turks, Mongols, and Kievan Rus, have shaped world history. Slavophilia, inspired in part by the literature of Fyodor Dostoevsky, articulates a future distinctive from western secular liberalism and socialism. Such assertions, associated with historic culture, translate into arguments in favour of a special destiny for Russia in the present.

A perceived history of decline can lead to the transformation of politics. This is most manifest among the nations that saw themselves to have fallen behind European states militarily during the 19th century. In Japan, after the Warring States period (1467–1568) and the long peace of the Tokugawa period (1603–1868), although there were several intertwined philosophical movements among Kokugaku, Shintō, and Buddhist scholars, Confucianism was prominent through the work of figures such as Itō Jinsai (1627–1705), Arai Hakuseki (1657–1725), and Ogyū Sorai (1666–1728), challenged by Andō Shōeki (1703–1762), and redefined for modern times by Fukuzawa Yukichi (1835–1901) and Nakae Chōmin (1847–1901) among others.

The necessity of change was accepted, however, because of the acknowledgement that although Japan historically had been successful as a state it could not compete with European powers. Fascination with the West became the norm. Interest in the history of political thought became European political thought on the grounds that this translated into national power and continued independence. Japan was opened to foreigners in 1853. The emperor was restored as the head of state in 1868 (Meiji Restoration) to prevent Japan from itself becoming a subject territory. The defeat of Russia in the 1904–5 war for the control of Manchuria and Korea confirmed that the Japanese had met their goal. In future decades they would seek to go beyond it by turning Japan into the dominant empire in Asia, which led in turn to the horrors of the Second Sino-Japanese war (1937–45), the Asia–Pacific War, and on to Hiroshima and Nagasaki.

China experienced the effects of relative military weakness directly during the Opium Wars against Britain (1839–42) and France (1856–60). That a state on the other side of the globe could crush with such ease a large state in Asia with a long history of civilization and independence had ramifications that continue to dictate attitudes to politics and history in China. The point has frequently been made—most recently by Youngmin Kim in *A History of Chinese Political Thought* (2018)—that Chinese political thought was distinctive because of the ancient Chinese statesman and philosopher Confucius (born Kǒng Qiū, 551–479 BCE), and the Confucianism that resulted from the study of his ideas. While this is true in the most general of senses we need to avoid reducing Sinosphere thinkers to monoliths. Across East Asia highly creative thinkers generation after generation engaged critically with the Confucian canon, whether the older *five classics* or the newer canon of the *four books* and Zhu Xi's neo-Confucian commentaries.

It is possible to generalize by arguing that the Confucian *four books* made canonical during the Southern Song dynasty (1127–1279) had a message that became a cultural force. They taught self-cultivation and governance through the operation of the networks of individual, family, and state working together. The importance of avoiding conflict and of peaceful resolution of difficulties can be compared with the antagonistic relationships, for example, between feudal lords and kings in Europe, from which can be traced institutions of representative government. Social networks operating in accordance with Confucian principles have been seen behind the Ming (1368–1644) and Qing (1636–1912) dynasties. The actual operation of Confucian and neo-Confucian philosophy in practice was infinitely more nuanced and complex, as becomes evident from the examination of Ogyū Sorai (1666–1728), who transformed traditional teachings in the hope of creating more stable government for the common good.

It is a mistake too to argue that historically being Chinese and living in social harmony became synonyms. It was the case, for example, that during the Ming period being Chinese became associated with a particular ethnicity. Legalism always justified violence when deemed necessary to maintain society. The key conclusion, however, is that the centralized state active in the life and culture of its citizens characteristic of communist China in the 20th and 21st centuries has been a European import. As in the case of Japan, there was a turn to Europe because the history of political thought taught states how to maintain themselves and a great divergence with respect to military power had occurred. At the same time, it has always been obvious that the notion of being 'European' or 'western' is complicated not least because the largest religion in the West was an import from the East and because of western debts to Arab and Indian astronomy, mathematics, and philosophy in addition to Chinese technology. When the term 'the West' is used numerous such borrowings have to be borne in mind.

What is the history of political thought?

Histories of political thought as sacred, tragic, nationalistic, and utopian can readily be identified through time. The history of political thought as an academic discipline, however, emerged in the 1960s as a rebellion against what might be termed hero and villain studies. Historians of political thought were critical of 'presentism', the reading into the past of contemporary debates on the assumption that the same questions were being studied over and over through history. They equally sought to avoid 'prolepsis', the anachronistic reading of historic books as if they were taking a stand on issues that in fact would have made no sense to their authors, such as whether they were democrats, supported human rights, or, these days, would have used Twitter or taken a view on whether Amazon/Google ought to pay more tax.

Histories of nations, churches, or moral communities have always been written to vindicate contemporary opinions, leaders, or institutions. In such narratives, the good, associated with whatever is being defended, gradually prevails against deluded critics. Today we can still find teleological historical writing, sometimes termed Whig history, in which, for example, a particular nation or religion emerges into the sunlight or a particular set of political values wins the laurel. In rejecting such approaches, the history of political thought provides an account of past ideas that is more accurate and more revealing because it is less judgemental. The actual circumstances of ideological battle can be reconstructed so that the dilemmas faced and choices made can be better explained and appreciated. The result is straightforwardly a more nuanced and useful interpretation of the human past.

The appearance of the history of political thought as a discipline must be understood against a background of catastrophic 20th-century global wars and genocide. The Nazis established across Europe more than 15,000 concentration camps dedicated to the genocide of Jews, Roma, and homosexuals, and to the employment of all of these groups, in addition to prisoners of war, as slave labour in the service of the German war economy. The erection, maintenance, and perpetuation of among the most monstrous instruments of human slaughter in history were the product of a political ideology justified by a history of ideas. For Nazis such as Adolf Hitler and Alfred Rosenberg the German people were a super race of Aryans. Aryans had been under attack from baser peoples, especially Semites, since the time of the Punic Wars between Aryan Rome and Semitic Carthage. Christianity had weakened the Germanic peoples, whose bloodlines were becoming impure, as evidenced by the rule of the Slavic peoples across the East. The natural hierarchy of races faced an unprecedented challenge in the form of Judaeo-Bolshevism, the ideology that had led from Marxism to Leninism and Trotskyism, which had caused the Russian Revolution, and which was likely to overrun the globe unless a crusade was initiated against it.

There was nothing new about ideologically justified atrocity in European history. From 1095 to 1453 crusaders had fought against Islam. Being on crusade to regain the Holy Land and save the Eastern Roman/Byzantine Empire entailed being 'marked by the Cross'. Christians in times of Reformation justified the killing of other Christians on the grounds of saving the soul of the murdered for Christ. The 20th century was no different. The British, during the Second Anglo-Boer War between 1900 and 1902, had employed a scorched earth policy to prevent Boer guerrillas from supplying themselves. Women and children saw their farms destroyed and were corralled into cramped camps where they lacked food and frequently succumbed to disease. During the First World War mass and mechanized warfare resulted in 40 million killed or wounded. Up to 1.5 million Armenians died at the hands of Ottoman forces between 1915 and 1923. In Soviet Russia Gulags had been established as early as 1919 to house opponents of the regime. In time Stalin turned the Gulags into a system of mass incarceration and slave labour. Approximately 14 million passed through the Gulags between 1929 and Stalin's death in 1953. Across the earth, between 1939 and 1945, the Second World War saw 75 million die, with the majority being civilians from genocide, bombs, starvation, and pestilence; and the Holocaust defies comparison.

Twentieth-century politics are the general context for understanding the emergence of the history of political thought as a field. Key texts that proved influential in the subject, not least because they were later accused of being infused with anachronistic readings of past ideas, included Friedrich Hayek's *The Road to Serfdom* (1944), Karl Popper's *The Open Society and its Enemies* (1945), Hannah Arendt's *The Origins of Totalitarianism* (1951), Jacob Talmon's *The Origins of Totalitarian Democracy* (1952), H. B. Acton's *The Illusion of the Epoch: Marxism-Leninism as a Philosophical Creed* (1955), and Raymond Aron's *The Opium of the Intellectuals* (1955). Numerous scholars working on the history of political thought from the 1950s followed such works in dedicating themselves to finding antidotes to Nazism, Fascism, or Stalinism. For the German-Jewish refugee Helmut Otto Pappe anyone who took seriously the works of the Genevan historian and political economist Jean-Charles-Léonard Simonde de Sismondi could never succumb to political fanaticism. A related claim was made by another exile from Nazi Germany, Jacob Peter Mayer, with regard to the French liberal theorist Alexis de Tocqueville. Some historians of political thought continue to argue that the central justification of the subject is its capacity to root out superstitious or extremist doctrines and provide a realist assessment of the dangers they pose.

The history of political thought as a discipline was created while attempts were ongoing to establish states legitimized by global ideologies in the aftermath of world war, be they Marx-inspired socialism/communism or liberal democracy/neoliberalism, all of which saw themselves to have satisfied human aspiration or at least established objective principles towards such a goal. This is important because historians of political thought have tended to be sceptical of global ideologies at the same time as they see themselves to be contributing to the prevention of future chaos and crisis. Many historians of political thought are adept at spotting the fault lines in contemporary political argument and the unconvincing and utopian assumptions that lie behind so many promises made by politicians and those who justify them ideologically. An example here is the work of Istvan Hont.

Hont revealed in his book *The Jealousy of Trade: International Competition and the Nation-State in Historical Perspective* (2005) that in the hands of someone like the 18th-century Scottish philosopher Adam Smith the analysis of politics at the level of the rise and fall of states could result in a comprehensive analysis of Europe and its prospects. Smith emphasized that war and luxury were responsible for the formation of modern states. In studying them, from China to Peru, Smith formulated phlegmatic and realistic strategies to engender peace and foster moderation. Being a realist in Smith's mould meant that you could be certain that you would not succeed; the point was to try nevertheless. For Hont, ambitiously following Smith, the history of political thought can make the human imagination identify tendencies in history while providing a brutally accurate assessment of current circumstances. Early warning systems can be established against fanaticism. Light can be shed upon the likely political future and the options open to communities in differing conditions.

The history of political thought can be adept at challenging interpretations of the past constructed by reifying the work of great men. Anthropological traditions which claim normative value in the present, such as the Thomist, Lockean, Spinozist, or Kantian, can be shown ultimately to lack historical validity. The work of Knud Haakonssen is illustrative in reconstructing the forgotten discipline of post-scholastic natural law, once a key component of university education across Europe. Historian Ann Thomson's work on European attitudes to North Africa, book history, translation, and cultural transfer during the Enlightenment era situates politics in contexts that complicate every assertion about meaning and influence. Among the most exciting developments in the history of political thought is the renewed attention paid to gender. Pathbreaking works have been published with titles such as *The Rule of Manhood: Tyranny, Gender and Classical Republicanism in England*, *Gendering the Renaissance Commonwealth*, and *Women and the History of International Thought*. Historians of political thought end up by creating complex, eclectic, and messy portraits of ideas closer to the reality of interacting human communities.

What do historians of political thought do?

Historians of political thought interrogate the social lives of historic communities in their own terms, studying their cultural practices, languages, and discourse to recover as far as possible people's own conversations about their lives. Historians of political thought seek to recover the problems and crises communities faced and argued about by looking at what was said, either directly in written form or through significant artefacts from surviving art and buildings to objects of everyday life. A move can be made from the recovery of historic meaning to its evaluation in the form of identifications of cause and effect; from the reconstruction of meaning we can also generate a sense of the political options open to individuals at specific points in time. Some historians of political thought take a further step and use the past to work out the lessons for the societies of the present.

The majority of historians of political thought study language, that is, the published or private utterances of historical figures who mounted opinions in political controversy. Sometimes the figures studied spent their lives writing and thinking as humanists, courtiers, philosophers, diplomats, or civil servants. Often political actors themselves recorded their views for public consumption or hidden personal reflection. Private individuals did the same and evidence of their thoughts is always revealing about past times. Every person counts from the point of view of most historians of political thought because meaning can be gleaned from the most meagre evidence or the basest of utterances. Equally, every piece of evidence from the past can be interrogated from the perspective of the history of political thought as revealing of ideological worlds and power relations within the studied communities. These tendencies have meant that historians of political thought since the 1960s have rejected the view of the past as an ongoing dialogue about the timeless questions of philosophy, the meaning of justice, happiness, courage, wisdom, and virtue. Historians of political thought now reject the notion of canonical figures in political thought. Those whose views before would have been deemed unworthy of recovery are now valued not only for shedding light on 'classic' texts but also for contributing to contemporary political discourses that historians want to reconstruct in order to make the past meaningful.

Leading figures in the history of European political theory—say Aristotle, Thomas Hobbes, and Jean-Jacques Rousseau—are studied in universities across the globe but often without any reference to history. The most common way of learning about major figures in the history of political thought is through reading primary texts, often in the form of a small section of a larger book. Few students of philosophy, for example, are ever asked to read the third and fourth parts of Hobbes's *Leviathan*.

They should. Hobbes deals with the fears of the imagination, with ghosts, and with ghouls. Few tutors in economics ask their students to read the third, fourth, and fifth books of Adam Smith's *Wealth of Nations* dealing with history, civil governance, taxation, and national defence. If Smith's work is examined from the perspective of the history of political thought a very different author can be seen, to be contrasted with the perceived founder of the science of economics. In an ideal world, if Smith was understood historically, a different economics might emerge too.

What counts as the history of political thought?

The issue of teaching practice raises the further question of how the history of political thought fits into existing academic disciplines. The point that needs to be made is that the history of political thought has yet to permeate many of the courses in which it is presumed to be taught. Major figures in the West have become members of a traditional canon stretching from Plato and Aristotle through to early modern giants and on to Immanuel Kant, Georg-Wilhelm-Friedrich Hegel, Karl Marx, John Stuart Mill, and so on to, say, Hannah Arendt and John Rawls. Such figures might well be taught in philosophy, politics, or history departments at university level. Their books are covered in what used to be termed Plato to Nato courses, more likely today to move from hunter-gatherer totemism to Trump, concerned with the history of ideas, in civics classes, or general courses concerned with the history of civilization and great thinkers. Once a tutor goes beyond the canon, however, problems arise. The question that is regularly posed can be framed as follows, with the name of the 'minor' figure changing: can Francis Hutcheson—himself considered by contemporaries to be one of the great philosophers of the 18th century—really be included in a list of Philosophers or Great Thinkers? What about Charles Fourier, entirely ignored in his time but, because of positive comments by Marx, now considered to have been a seminal figure in the history of socialism? Does a figure fit into disciplinary histories of philosophy or literature or international relations or political theory? Who should be 'in' and who should be 'out'?

The problem is compounded when national histories are considered. It suddenly matters whether Kant, who spent near the entirety of his life in what was then the city of Königsberg in Prussia and is now Kaliningrad in Russia, should be seen as a philosopher who was a Prussian, a German, a Pole, a Russian, a founder of liberalism, a cosmopolitan supporter of the French Revolution, an enemy to all forms of nationalism, or a racist anthropologist? The history of political thought is often badly taught in ahistorical survey courses that continue to fire pointless questions at dead philosophers. In Kant's case, scholars such as Ian Hunter have been recovering the reception of his work in his own time as a philosophical religion, shaped by Lutheran metaphysics, and in direct competition with the biblical–ecclesiastical religions. In restoring the theological context that governed the elaboration and reception of Kantian philosophy, this approach not only transforms Kant's moral law from a command of reason into a lifestyle choice, it also pushes Kant's law and politics across the border of the history of political thought and into the domains of ecclesiastical history and the history of metaphysics.

The attentive reader may already have noticed two things about the history of political thought. The first is that the canonical texts traditionally studied tend to have been written by men. The subject has always been seen to be among the most masculine. This perception has endured despite the brilliance of a long list of female historians of political thought. Taking the period from the mid-17th century to the French Revolution alone, Caroline Robbins's *The Eighteenth-Century Commonwealthman* (1959) transformed the field, Nannerl Keohane's *Philosophy and the State in France* (1980) has classic status, and Patricia James's research into Thomas Robert Malthus conducted in the 1970s and early 1980s remains unsurpassed. More recently our knowledge of the relationship between philosophy and politics in Hobbes, Pufendorf, Spinoza, and Leibniz has been transformed by the research of Fiammetta Palladini, Susan James, and Maria-Rosa Antognazza.

A similar list could be supplied for every subject and every period. More female political theorists too are being studied: examples from Europe to the end of the 18th century include the Neoplatonist Hipatia (360–415 CE), Christine de Pizan (1364–1430), Mary Astell (1666–1731), Émilie du Châtelet (1706–49), Catharine Macaulay (1731–91), Olympe de Gouges (1748–93), and Mary Wollstonecraft (1759–97). At the same time, if the encyclopedic *Cambridge History of Political Thought* volumes are considered, it is remarkable that Hannah Arendt is missing from the index of the book devoted to *Twentieth-Century Political Thought*. Despite this omission, Arendt is the subject of more doctoral dissertations and is currently receiving more scholarly attention than any other 20th-century thinker.

A similar point, naturally, can be made about politics itself. The claim has been made that when Maria Theresa became the sole female ruler of the Habsburg dominions, becoming archduchess of Austria and queen of Hungary and Croatia, an observer stated that she had become a man and ceased to be a woman. Even in contemporary monarchies the ruling monarch constitutionally tends to be a male. If a woman becomes queen, her husband is not referred to as a king but rather is given the title of 'prince'. Hence the husband of the former Dutch Queen Beatrix was Prince Klaus. The wife of the current Dutch King Willem Alexander has the title Queen Maxima, just as the wife of the former British monarch Edward VI was called Queen Elizabeth, significantly without a number after her name. You might think that this does not matter because most of us inhabit republics. Yet in republics there tends to be no male equivalent to the position of First Lady. We all know about the status of Michelle Obama or Melania Trump in the United States and Brigitte Macron in France. Most people, however, are unable to name the husband of the long-standing leader of Germany, Angela Merkel (Figure 6).

6. Pierre-Étienne Lesueur, *Club Patriotique de Femmes* (1792–4).

A second point is that the traditional history of the political thought canon and the major figures within it has tended to be European for the most part. Sometimes figures from the United States are added, such as the Founding Fathers Thomas Jefferson and James Madison. Why is this the case? Why has the history of political thought as standardly practised not focused on Confucius or Kautilya (375–283 BCE), the author of the Sanskrit treatise *Arthashastra* and chief adviser to the Emperor Chandragupta, who ruled the Mauryan Empire? Alternatively, why is the Arab scholar Ibn Khaldun not included, who was born in Tunis in 1332 CE and who composed the *Muqaddimah* or *Prolegomena*, which defined wellbeing in an Islamic state?

The western male canon has been the touchstone for the subject and remains dominant, but it is being challenged. Scholarship in the history of political thought has been 'Eurocentric' in the sense of dealing with ideas about politics generated in the Graeco-Roman Mediterranean that were then communicated across medieval and modern Europe. Such ideas were adopted in the Americas when they were colonized by Europeans and then across the entire world insofar as it was dominated by a militarily unchallengeable West. Eurocentrism is, however, now being questioned and corrected with an unparalleled increase in studies of non-western traditions of political thought in addition to work concerned with political thought in relatively neglected eastern Europe. Vocal calls are also being made for what is called global social and political thought, itself with a global history. The question of what might be 'global' about political thought, why it might be a good thing and how far it can necessarily challenge Eurocentrism will be returned to later in this book. The history of European political thought continues to be worth studying not least because of its global ramifications. It must never be defined rigidly, recognizing its diversity, hybrid nature, and historical dependence upon other parts of the earth.

We continue to learn so much from the world beyond the West. Kautilya's defence of sacred monarchy is illustrative not least because, although such a doctrine has ceased to exist in India, it continues to be associated with the Papacy and to thrive in such countries as Japan, the United Kingdom, Thailand, Jordan, and North Korea. Interest in non-state forms of politics necessarily entails stepping beyond European frameworks. The ongoing and vital fascination with natural living sustainably and closer to nature demands the same. W. C. Woodbridge's 1827 *Moral and Political Chart of the World* depicting regions of 'savages', 'barbarians', 'half-civilized', and 'civilized' has been consigned to history (Figure 7).

Discovering the history of political thought

Since planning this book I have been asking lots of people from different parts of the world how they came to be interested in the

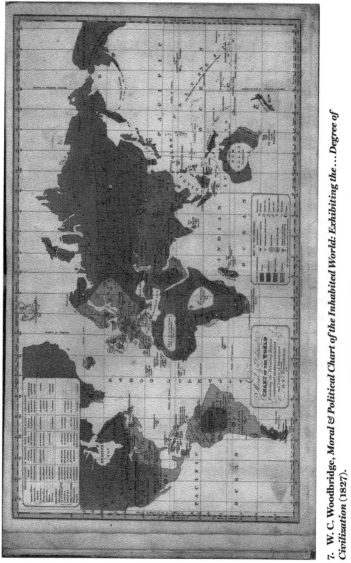

7. W. C. Woodbridge, *Moral & Political Chart of the Inhabited World: Exhibiting the ... Degree of Civilization* (1827).

history of political thought. The answer tends to be by taking general courses in the humanities or social sciences in which a European canon of political ideas is identified and studied, encompassing, for example, Hobbes, Locke, Montesquieu, Rousseau, Burke, Kant, Herder, Hegel, Weber, Meinecke, Isaiah Berlin, Leo Strauss, and Michel Foucault. One regular comment was that there were no adequate textbooks. Several students read George Sabine's *A History of Political Theory* (1937), Arthur O. Lovejoy's *The Great Chain of Being* (1936), Karl Popper's *The Open Society and its Enemies* (1945), Leo Strauss's *History of Political Philosophy* (1963), and, more than any other recently published book, Quentin Skinner's *The Foundations of Modern Political Thought* (1978).

One of the great issues identified over and over was the legacy of the Enlightenment for the 20th-century and 21st-century world. This in turn raised the question of the extent to which the Enlightenment could be said to define 'the West' and its politics. Many students were inspired by reading translations of Max Horkheimer's and Theodor W. Adorno's *Dialectic of Enlightenment* (*Dialektik der Aufklärung*) (1947). In numerous cases reference was made to remarkable tutors who might have been educated abroad. Some of them had translated the texts being studied. For others, understanding their own societies necessitated knowledge of, for example, the triumph of Stalin in Russia or Mao in China and, more broadly, the intellectual origins of socialism/communism.

In all countries, liberal philosophers such as Raymond Aron or Isaiah Berlin introduced a large number of students to the history of political thought. The intellectual historian John W. Burrow recalled that in the early 1950s he found the subject by picking up John Neville Figgis's *From Gerson to Grotius* (1916). This occurred around the same time as Burrow heard wireless talks by Berlin on the subject of 'Freedom and its Betrayal', so captivating that he sat on the floor while listening and took notes. Many readers or listeners found Berlin's argument compelling that Soviet communism needed to be feared. This was because its foreign policy, just as aggressive as that of the western liberal states, was buttressed by a powerful teleological view of a history, which taught the inevitability of communism's economic and military victory over capitalism.

Leo Strauss became highly acclaimed too after the publication of his *On Tyranny* (1948) and *Persecution and the Art of Writing* (1952). It was Strauss, for example, who, not without irony, developed something of a cult following in both the United States and communist China. Part of the reason was that neo-Confucians in China enjoyed seeking out hidden messages in sacred texts awaiting scholars sufficiently gifted and eminent to decipher them. This approach accorded with Strauss's search for esoteric writing in major philosophical texts, which will be explained later in this book. In short, Strauss could be presented in China as a neo-Confucian philosopher despite himself.

Ultimately the dedicated students in different parts of the world discovered John Pocock's works. Pocock's case is an interesting one because he was brought up in New Zealand. Like so many others, he came to the history of political thought through Sabine's summary book. Pocock later made the point that whatever Sabine was doing he was not practising the history of political thought. In his early 20s Pocock heard Karl Popper give the Canterbury lectures that became *The Open Society and its Enemies*. These contained a particular attack upon philosophies characterized by what Popper called 'historicism'. What Popper meant by historicism was the reduction of history to fixed laws of progress from which there could be no dissent, and he rightly saw such historicism as leading through non-refutability to tyranny.

The Second World War was at the point of what became the Cold War, and Popper, Pocock discovered, was going about declaring that the western allies should, at least in principle, declare war on the Soviet Union. At this point Pocock noticed that Popper began committing the sin of prolepsis, reading the problems of the present into the past and judging past authors for the stand they were held to have taken, entirely without historical justification. Popper blamed Plato for Hegel and Hegel for both Hitler and Stalin, constructing while making his verdicts a list of 'safe' liberal thinkers whose work would not lead to tyranny. According to Pocock, Popper was right about history conceptually but entirely wrong about history as he constructed it as a narrative. Pocock realized—and so did Quentin Skinner at around the same time—that you can play language games with past texts in political thought which may have nothing at all to do with the historical reality. Pocock thought that as long as you recognized that that was what you were doing, thereby avoiding claims about history, this was a valid philosophical enterprise. The likelihood, however, was that you would be led to what he called 'the history game'. Both Pocock and Skinner preferred to get the history right before they played games with politics.

It is important to recognize that older approaches to the history of political thought that prevailed immediately after the Second World War are unlikely to be returned to. It was then argued that improving the world—by reading Sismondi or Tocqueville and avoiding Plato, Hegel, or Marx for example—was as simple as providing the books and talking about their content with your friends, students, co-workers, and peers. In the aftermath of many of the worst experiences in human history, such naivety was commonplace. People did not want war. They were not naturally selfish. They wanted to promote the general good of all, across social classes and national borders. Everyone was capable of acting rationally and being swayed by reason. Alternatively, from the perspective of behaviourist social sciences and especially economics, there was no point in reflecting upon the past because human nature was constantly selfish and interest-maximizing. The role of science was to curb behaviour in the cases where selfishness went against the common good.

We live in a very different time. In some forms of state, interest in the history of political thought essentially depends on whether a crisis is seen to be being lived through or to be on the horizon. In many forms of state, attitudes towards the history of political thought depend on what people are allowed to read and how far they can think for themselves. In the West neither neo-Kantian claims about universally rational values nor the portrayal of humans by Behavioural Economics as rational utility maximizers any longer convince. The study of the history of political thought too has been transformed. As rarely before, it is under attack. There is evidence—and the issue will be discussed in the final chapter of this book—that the subject is facing a time of crisis. Globally there has been a marked turn against historical studies that are directly or indirectly critical of nationalist political narratives, manufactured political consensuses, or social-media driven moral crusades. Marketing pervades politics and social life, and accurate history is the enemy of propaganda. Politicians are much less reflective and much less informed about past politics.

The same can be said about the denizens of social media. Part of the reason lies in the tendency for electors in representative democracies to be willing to vote for simple messages of hope and optimistic promises of speedy gratification. Another lies in the more general narrative of inevitable economic growth and progress, which leads many to reject the past as inferior to the present and therefore unlikely to have any meaning for us today. This book provides a guide for the general reader and the student, those who want to know about the main approaches in our time, where they came from, how they have been criticized, and, above all, *why they matter.*

Chapter 3
The history of political thought and Marxism

The origins of Marx and of Marxism

Marxism became in the 20th century the most global philosophy ever encountered in addition to being the most ambitious and, for its devotees at least, the most scientific. In order to understand Marxism we have to go back to Karl Marx, the émigré from Prussian Trier who had left Cologne, Paris, and Brussels because his pro-revolutionary journalism had been condemned by the authorities and ended up in London from 1849. He famously composed subsequent contributions to what became the science of historical materialism in the reading room of the British Museum. Marx's works, until his death in 1883, and those of his close friend, patron, and collaborator, the industrialist Friedrich Engels, who had come to Marx's attention because of his book *The Condition of the Working Class in England* (1844), justified revolution through a new philosophy. The philosophy emerged from a reading of European history, concluding that the ideas behind the history had failed and needed to be changed, in all likelihood by violence. Understanding what Marx and Engels saw themselves to be doing means reconstructing their view of Europe's failure as a continent with the then most militarily dominant states on earth.

Marx and Engels accepted that by the end of the 18th century the progress of commerce had made European states more powerful than others in history, in part because of the modern system of public credit that allowed them to borrow vast sums on the promise of future tax revenues. These resources could then be used to pay for the vast armies and navies necessary to fight wars, supported by increasingly sophisticated military technology. Marx and Engels rejected the argument that commerce was a force for peace and politeness by bringing the nations of the globe together in trade. Rather, it was the case that European states sought ever more trade through the pursuit of empire, taking control of the markets of smaller states both within Europe and beyond.

Adam Smith was a hero for Marx because of the systematic nature of his *Wealth of Nations* (1776), combining conjectural historical analysis with the history of politics, morals, and the economy. Marx was attracted above all, however, by Smith's revelation of the real mechanisms of British society in his assault upon the empire as a 'mercantile system'. This was Smith's term for a political-economic system that emerged from a governing relationship between rich merchants and politicians who passed legislation for their own profit rather than for the good of all. What became Marxism was yet another attempt to remove the possibility of the rule of mercantile systems from earth. Understanding how means returning briefly to Smith's contemporaries and to what happened during and after the French Revolution.

Like his contemporaries Montesquieu, François Quesnay, David Hume, Anne-Robert-Jacques Turgot, and Rousseau, Smith believed the study of societies in every stage of history to be vital in understanding what the future was likely to be and in combating dangers, from repeating the fall of Rome to rekindling religious extremism. All of these men were certain that Europe was different from past societies because of commerce. Yet they were equally certain that the study of what we would now call global history and thought was necessary in order to appreciate the European predicament, to turn commerce pacific, and to put an end to the lust for empire and addiction to the consumption of luxury goods. It was important to have knowledge of the different theologies of the world to prevent the recurrence of religious warfare. These were themes of Montesquieu's *Lettres persanes* (*Persian Letters*), employing the ruse of Muslims travelling across Europe to reveal the nature of the European self through the eyes of 'the other'. It was accepted too that to understand commerce and empire it was necessary to study the great trading cities of the past, from Tyre and Carthage, Ragusa and Genoa, to Venice, and the empires of the past from the Achaemenid to the Mughal and the Ottoman. In particular, European jurists were fascinated by China as a model of a stable state that had avoided war and division. Their ultimate goal, which they recognized to be unachievable, was to create policies in accordance with what they called the good of humanity as a whole, being formulated ideally by 'friends of mankind'.

If there was an opinion that was shared across all of the philosophers and jurists across Europe in the 18th century it was that the British state was unlikely to survive. Britain was accepted as being the foremost commercial state. It had also experienced religious-inspired civil war in the previous century. Britain was identified by Montesquieu as the freest state in history. He called it, in his influential masterpiece *De l'esprit des lois* (*The Spirit of the Laws*, 1748), a republic hiding beneath the form of a monarchy. What Montesquieu meant was that the Georgian monarchs who ruled Britain had powers limited by the House of Commons and the House of Lords. The control by representatives of national finances was a republican notion. Hence Britain was a mixed government, a hybrid of monarchy, aristocracy, and democracy. It was equally the most indebted state ever known, with politics lurching from crisis to crisis. The collapse of the state was widely anticipated after the Seven Year's War (1757–63). When Britain was defeated by the North American former-colonists, supported by France, Spain, and the Dutch Republic, the long-held view that Britain was in decline appeared to have been confirmed. By the end of the 1780s, being near bankrupt with a king, ruling a divided society, almost every commentator would have predicted revolution would occur in Britain rather than in France.

The revolution that commenced at Paris in 1789 is widely considered the most important event in the history of political thought. It was from reflection upon the course of the French Revolution that Marx first formulated his radical political tactics. Marx was certain that the French Revolution and the course it took was the touchstone of political analysis and the key to moving humanity to higher stages of life in socialist and communist communities. Understanding why Marx came to such a conclusion—of singular import to humans across the globe especially in the 20th century—requires returning to the way events in France shocked contemporaries and altered perceptions of politics. When Edmund Burke published his *Reflections on the Revolution in France* in November 1790, critical of events at Paris, he was certain that the revolution was going to fail. Any state, Burke argued, that abolished the institutions on which society depended, the monarchy, aristocracy, and church, was bound to become ever more violent until it collapsed. Burke was widely portrayed as a prophet as the Revolution destabilized. Yet he considered himself to have been wrong. Rather than declining France became ever-more powerful as a state as the 1790s progressed.

Burke died despondent in 1797 because a state had been created that defied what to Burke were the laws of politics proven by history. France, lacking stable institutions, and making Britain's economic plight look rosy by comparison, had created a vast republican empire so popular as to make the Holy Roman Emperor Charles V envious. Burke was frightened that a new world had been created of fanatic ideological politics in which people would fight to the death for liberty. Liberty appeared to have become more important than life. Burke saw ceaseless turbulence and war ahead as the people turned against their rulers. It is important to recognize that in the final years of his life Burke found a solution to the problem in war to the death against republican France by Britain. In other words, a patriotic and nationalistic ideology had to be generated capable of battling against the republican cosmopolitans who believed they were fighting for the universal rights of all peoples and justice for all mankind.

When France ceased to be a republic and became an empire ruled by a single sovereign many observers of politics and history were relieved. The French Republic that had defied political logic for so many years was once more on an explicable path, being yet another popular state whose citizens welcomed a Caesar figure in the form of Napoleon Bonaparte. The most influential revolutionary theorist, Sieyès, who had railed against the injustices of aristocratic dominion under the Old Regime, was made a count by Bonaparte and given extensive lands. Sieyès ceased to write about politics, turning his back on his own philosophy. Other republican radicals, such as Thomas Paine or Mary Wollstonecraft, observed the course of the French Revolution with growing disdain. Wollstonecraft detested the politics of Burke in the 1790s, but when she died in 1797, giving birth to Mary Shelley, she was cynical about the forms of oppression that she was certain prevailed in all states.

Paine lived until 1809, increasingly convinced that the terror that had ruined the French Revolution had spread to the United States of America. Paine had dreamed of sister republics living in peace and harmony. By the early 1800s he was advising his friend President Thomas Jefferson to purchase Louisiana from a bankrupt French state. The United States too had to become larger and more powerful, generating commercial revenues to defend itself in war, just like the European forms of state from which the Founding Fathers had differentiated their polity. This meant that in terms of political thought the early 19th century yielded depressing truths about the likely future. The French Republic and its promise of making the world more just and egalitarian by putting into practice natural rights had altogether failed. The new model state was Britain, portrayed positively as a liberal archetype of liberty and moderation, but negatively as a polity addicted to war and empire. For critics the British people supported their rulers because of the exploitation of nations abroad, especially beyond Europe. They were also loyal because of their xenophobic nationalism, unleashed during the wars against the French Republic and Bonaparte.

If a combination of nationalism and a mercantile system of corrupt trading companies translated into proficiency at war, the future of politics was bleak. Philosophers from Hume and Kant to Hegel acknowledged that at the end of the 18th century superstition and enthusiasm, terms used to describe dangerous theological fanatics who had thrived in time of Reformation, had translated from religion to politics. Enlightenment policies dedicated to preventing the recurrence of the forms of religious warfare that had shattered Europe in the 16th and 17th centuries were ceasing to function. Three solutions presented themselves to the end of Enlightenment. The first was to create a science of legislation capable of defining the public good through rational laws. The second was to reform liberal polities so that they might combine civil and political liberty with pacific internationalism and free trade. The third was to abolish politics altogether, in the sense of the institutional structures that were held responsible for organizing social life. In the history of political thought, the first two aspirations led to the work of a stream of liberal philosophers through the 19th century, all of whom wanted to create societies immune to mercantile systems, the excesses of empire, and bigoted nationalism. The third response led to Marx and Engels.

Marx's philosophy

The pull of Marxism had the greatest impact upon the writing of the history of political thought through the 20th century. Even critics defined their own work against the Marxist creed. Although there are now fewer devotees of historical materialism, it may well come back into fashion. The lure is extremely powerful because it promises so much and condemns capitalist societies so profoundly. Marx claimed to have turned history into a subject as objective as any study of the natural or physical world. History became directly relevant to politics in justifying the most ambitious revolutionary programme for human improvement. The end point of the revolution was to make humans live peaceably without politics, in the hyper-productive communist societies where people enjoyed leisure and fulfilment without the oppressive overlords of the dominating state.

Many historians of political ideas up to the end of the 1980s were Marxists. They had been attracted by a philosophy which promised to heal the ills of society and predict the future, being the transition from the unjust capitalist system to one in which the labour of every person was fairly rewarded (socialism) and ultimately to a society where the needs of every person would be satisfied (communism). Historical analysis and societal progress could be combined in a straightforward fashion, yielding real dividends in the form of concrete policy presented as indisputable, being in accordance with the science of historical materialism. Much work in the history of political thought has derived from the refutation of Marxist approaches to the subject. Historians of political thought have always engaged, for example, with the question of rights of resistance, ultimately whether revolution is the best means of changing a state or starting a new community from scratch.

Yet the power of Marxist thought is evident in the resemblance between Marxism and doctrines that claim to be most resolutely opposed to it. Modern-day neoliberal free marketeers, for example, who have imbibed the 'laws' of economics and see no alternative to unfettered capitalism, themselves peddle a version of the Marxist narrative in their refusal to see alternatives, their demand that every problem needs to be seen in global terms, their certainty that what they do is backed by science and that they alone are right.

Marx asserted that increasing the forces of production, land and labour, which created capital, was the goal of every human community throughout history. The use of the forces of production was governed by existing social relations of production. A dominant social relation of production defined particular societies. As such, societies might be slave-based, feudal, or capitalist, depending on which social relation, master and slave, lord and peasant, or capitalist and free labourer, could be seen to be dominant. The dominant social relation of production governed the leading ideas of a society so that the operation of human minds, the realm of ideas, could be read off the material forces in control. This view harked back to Marx's critique of Hegel, asserting that idealism had to be rejected as a philosophical basis for the study of human societies.

According to Marx the operation of the body ultimately determined the workings of the human mind. Hegel's genius had been to make sense of ideological forces operating through human history. Marx took the further necessary step of turning Hegel's study of the ideological forces of a society materialist, by revealing the material forces determining each and every ideology. Marx saw himself to have turned a chaotic analysis of ultimately random ideas and ideologies into pure science. In any society, once the dominant relation of production had been identified, functioning as the base of the society, the supportive superstructure of philosophy, art, and politics could be read off. So could the critical voices demanding revolutionary change towards a higher relation of production, bringing greater mastery of the forces of production for humanity. Once these critical voices were translated into revolutionary movements able to take power, a time of crisis would see the replacement of the old relation of production with the higher form, bringing with it a newly dominant ideological superstructure supportive of the new relation of production.

In the 20th century, being able to analyse scientifically the evils of the capitalist relation of production and preach the benefits of the socialist alternative, to be realized through the replacement of the bourgeoisie with the dominion of the proletariat in society, proved especially appealing. Was it not obvious that, as Lenin put it, the rule of the soviets (workers' councils) plus electrification would bring better times for all? Marxism was attractive to high-minded moralists and cosmopolitans, those who foresaw a better future for humanity without national borders, want, war, or division. The battle against the ruling capitalist bourgeoisie would everywhere be bloody, such was their authority and the resources at their command. Yet history was moving in a single direction, the creation of a better world was both inevitable and logical for everyone, so that to die in the struggle might well be the most justifiable of sacrifices (Figure 8).

Marx and political thought

Studying the history of political ideas from a Marxist perspective might appear to be rudimentary labour. Ideas about politics in any society depended upon the condition of the relations of production. The economic analysis of the precise circumstances of the currently dominant form of production revealed how this mode of production had evolved and the extent of the injustice at its foundations. Having undertaken such analysis, political ideas were either supportive of the existing relations of production or revolution towards a higher mode. One consequence of the popularity of Marxist approaches was the flourishing of economic history in the 20th century.

8. Walter Crane, *International Solidarity of Labour* (1889).

The history of political thought did, however, have a further role to play in the process of the improvement of humanity. Marx had been vague about the exact transition mechanism from capitalism to socialism. He had at first predicted, in his *Communist Manifesto* of 1848 for example, that revolutions were straightforward affairs. Feudalism died at the point where the bourgeoisie took control of politics, which Marx anticipated with the liberal-nationalist revolutions that shook Europe during this year. The bourgeoisie would in turn be overthrown by the proletarians, who would institute a social organization based on work rather than profit. In practice things proved more complicated. Rather than bringing the final victory of the bourgeoisie necessary for the next stage of historical evolution to prepare itself, the 1848 revolutions saw the return of seemingly feudal reactionaries such as Louis Napoleon Bonaparte, elected by French peasants to bring a return to the glory days of his emperor uncle. In his *The Class Struggles in France, 1848–1850*, originally published as a series of articles in the *Neue Rheinische Zeitung* in 1850, Marx, always adept at self-justification, argued that although history played tricks with present politics, the 1848 revolutions had indeed said farewell to feudalism and brought the rule of the bourgeoisie, even if their dominion had not translated into practical politics. Louis Napoleon Bonaparte had to rule for the bourgeoisie even if he and his peasant power base pretended otherwise.

Marx's solution was elegant. At the same time, it made the practice of politics open to scrutiny, becoming a fluid element of Marxist science. Marx remained vague about the surest route to socialism. Uncertainty about what became known as praxis was compounded by disputes about where the collapse of capitalism would first occur and how the revolution would spread to different countries or continents. Marx had confidently predicted in all of his early works that capitalism would collapse where it was most advanced, for the good reason that its limitations would be most manifest and the socialist opposition most highly organized. As the capitalist states, especially Britain, seemed to become more stable as the 19th century progressed and as socialist movements thrived in places where capitalism and urbanization was less well established, such as Russia, question marks were raised. In a letter to the Russian socialist Vera Zasulich of March 1881 Marx speculated that non-capitalist societies like Russia might move directly from feudalism to socialism because of the strength of the village commune. Once socialism was established it would then spread to the more advanced economies of Europe. Different answers to such questions, from Stalin's doctrine of 'socialism in one country' to Trostky's notion of permanent revolution until socialism was universally embraced, divided Marxists throughout the 20th century.

The most intense divisions within Marxism concerned practical revolutionary politics. Revolution might occur through an organized party acting as a proxy or vanguard for the massed ranks of the proletariat, taking control of the institutions of the state and holding onto them by violence if necessary until socialist society could be made real. Taking money from capitalists themselves to support the revolutionary vanguard was even deemed legitimate. This was why Lenin was happy to take funds from the German state to enable his Bolshevik party to organize revolution in Russia, ultimately defeating the more democratic or liberal-minded Mensheviks in overturning the tsarist state after the popular uprising of October 1917.

Vanguards of dedicated cadres, professional revolutionaries who would do whatever it took to facilitate the establishment of a workers' state or socialism, were accepted as a transition mechanism in the breakdown of capitalism. One problem with this approach to politics, increasingly termed Leninism, was that having such a vanguard was tantamount to accepting that there was something 'wrong' with the workers themselves, because they lacked consciousness of their historic destiny and refused to rebel. Another more deadly problem was that the fanatic Leninists, once they had taken control of the state, refused to dismantle it by handing it over to the workers, preferring to remain in power themselves and establish a new autocracy.

György Lukács, a well-educated and noble-born Hungarian Marxist, outlined a different plan for the establishment of socialism in his book *History and Class Consciousness (Geschichte und Klassenbewußtsein)* of 1923. Lukács favoured a democratic union of the proletariat and the peasantry exercising dictatorial power in the early phases of the revolution until the full dictatorship of the proletariat could be maintained. By 1923 events in the now Soviet Union had begun to dictate the 'truth' of Marxism to acolytes. The ruling body, the Comintern, censored Lukács for heresy. His works became foundational for the branch of Marxism that later emerged in criticism of developments in the Soviet Union, known as Western Marxism.

Speculation about what Marxist politics ought to be made the link clear between Marxism and the history of political thought into the 1980s. Students had to make a decision as to whether they were Marxists and then what branch of Marxist philosophy they would devote themselves to. Louis Althusser's works were considered essential reading in this process from his *For Marx (Pour Marx,* 1965) (1969) and *Reading Capital (Lire 'le Capital',* 1965) (1970), written with his students Étienne Balibar and Jacques Rancière, to his *Politics and History: Montesquieu, Rousseau, Marx (Montesquieu, la politique et l'histoire,* 1959–70). Histories of Marxist thought were popular too, especially those of Herbert Marcuse, Leszek Kolakowski, and Shlomo Avineri.

The sheer intellectual power of Marxist doctrine has to be acknowledged, especially for the generation educated in the 1920s and 1930s, when capitalism appeared to be on its knees. Although the linkage of socialism with tyranny and Caesar-figures was acknowledged from the time of Stalin's Moscow Trials (1936–8), the Soviet model nevertheless offered an alternative to the spread of fascist dictatorship across Europe. The sacrifices made by the Russian people during the Great Patriotic War against Hitler's Germany underlined the sense of contrast. Even when evidence was revealed of the brutalities of the Soviet Union, including mass famine and the slaughter or ostracism of even minor critics of the regime, the fact that in a short period of time Russia had industrialized and strengthened itself to the point of being able to defeat Nazi Germany made it attractive to would-be socialists and reformers. That it was backed up by a philosophy claiming certainty about the future course of history and the inescapable improvement of humanity ensured that it appealed to gullible young idealists.

Figures at both ends of the political spectrum acknowledged Marxism's force. Many who ultimately defined themselves against Marxism went through a communist phase, including Popper. Hugh Trevor Roper, never a friend to the left, acknowledged the appeal of Marxism and the skills of the historians whose research it inspired. In the 1920s the philosopher and archaeologist R. G. Collingwood identified Marx as being of great importance in his *Speculum Mentis* (1924) because 'all thought exists for the sake of action'. In his later *Autobiography* (1939) he recalled that during this phase of his life he praised Marx as 'a fighting philosopher' to be compared to the weaker vessels that dominated the universities, divorced from society and who turned politics into a debating club.

It was commonplace for young men and women with a moral conscience, such as James H. Burns at Aberdeen in the 1940s, to join the local Communist Party. In Burns's case he moved from communism to Catholicism. When the undergraduate Elie Kedourie arrived at the London School of Economics in the late 1940s he was welcomed by Alfred Sherman, subsequently a grandee of the Tory Party. Sherman immediately took him to a meeting, which turned out to be a recruitment forum for the Communist Party. All of these figures later became deeply opposed to Marxism. While their support amounted to a passing phase, many others continued to accept Marxism as the key to their intellectual identities. It was no surprise that the renowned 'History of Ideas Unit' at the Australian National University at Canberra, which flourished through the 1980s, was directed by the sometime Marxist Eugene Kamenka. Marx has always had powerful and sometimes brilliant defenders, such as the Oxford philosopher Gerry Cohen, whose *Karl Marx's Theory of History: A Defence* appeared in 1978.

The difficulty of refuting Marx

If the influence of Marxism among historians of political thought is hard to underestimate, the difficulty of refuting such a philosophy also has to be accepted. One danger for historians of political thought was that in rejecting a Marxist framework of understanding they were identifying themselves as antiquarians, uninterested in turning the history of political thought into a force for social change. This can be seen in the work of the influential classicist turned historian of political thought and political theorist Ernest Barker. In 1927 Barker was appointed to a new Rockefeller-funded chair in Political Science at Cambridge and remained in post for eleven years. He taught the two historical papers founded by John Seeley and this led to two books, *Reflections on Government* (1942) and *Principles of Social and Political Theory* (1951). These continued Barker's assault on modern dictatorship, which he identified in Nazi Germany and Soviet Russia. His critique had been formulated many years before.

Barker was heavily influenced by the legal historian F. W. Maitland's Ford Lectures at Oxford of 1897 entitled 'Township and Borough'. These followed the German jurist Otto von Gierke in identifying the formation of associations as key to

European history. Barker translated part of Gierke's *Genossenschaftsrecht* as *Natural Law and the Theory of Society* in 1934 and in an introduction attacked the fanatic nationalist/racist groups he saw in Germany and in Italy, and the class-based groups in Soviet Russia. Such groups, Barker argued, were the production of an exclusive and bigoted Roman-law influenced Romanticism to be contrasted with the diverse associations of English life, in turn the product of the law of equity and trusts. The English 'spirit of compromise' could, Barker argued in *The Political Thought of Plato and Aristotle* of 1906, be traced to Aristotle.

What did such arguments amount to? Barker was an apologist for the superiority of English life and culture at a time when it was under attack. He detested war and supported the government of Neville Chamberlain in appeasing Hitler. After the war he was worried about the control of the state over the individual through planning and attacked the reforms of the Labour government of 1945–51 on such grounds. Such stances, however grounded in scholarship and carefully formulated, came across as altogether utopian compared with the activism of Barker's student, the Marxist Harold Laski. After the First World War Laski had followed his supervisor in defending liberal pluralism. As Professor of Political Science at the London School of Economics from 1925 he changed his stance, moving towards Marxism in the form of a defence of Stalin and the Soviet Union from 1930. Laski inspired a generation of students through his lectures and ceaseless campaigning. Despite writing numerous tortuous books, subsequent influential figures on the left, such as Jawaharlal Nehru or Ralph Miliband, said that they owed an enormous amount to Laski, for whom ideas mattered in leading the history of political thought to justify societal transformation.

In 1938 R. G. Collingwood, having praised Marxists, concluded in his *The Principles of Art* that Marxism amounted ultimately neither to philosophy nor to history. Marxism needed to be understood as a religion with a creed, set of values, and prescribed system of conduct. This made Marxism as dangerous as the other contemporary political religion, fascism. A letter Collingwood wrote before he died is worth citing because it makes clear that the greatest challenge to the history of thought came from religion; theology had a capacity to make sense of the world for people susceptible to the peddling of compelling myths:

> I gave a diagnosis [of the Nazis and fascism more generally] in the *Autobiography*, but it was wrong. I tried there to give an account of them in Marxist terms, as class-war phenomena; but that was wrong—I now see them as *religious* phenomena: outcrops of pre-Christian religion in revolt against Christianity and therefore against civilization, which (as we understand it) is a corollary of Christianity.

Collingwood's point was repeated time after time in the post-war period. Marxism demanded quasi-religious devotion. Cadres were in actuality members of an evangelical church. Toleration was never to be expected. Battles with other sects occurred naturally, each portraying themselves as truly Marxist to be contrasted with the doctrinal heresies of others. The focus of the struggle at times gave the impression of being about the crushing of heresy and dissent from particular perspectives upon Marxism as much as the war against capitalism. As we will see, such attacks, in the hands of Reinhard Koselleck, drawing upon Carl Schmitt, coincided with an interpretation of the modern world as ideologically theological and therefore subject to periodic bouts of utopian fanaticism.

Marxism and Maoism

The actions of French-educated radical philosophers in the second half of the 20th century, who found themselves coming to power by revolution in China, Vietnam, and Cambodia, were inspired by a Catholic archbishop who lived in Louis XIV's France, François Fénelon. It was from Fénelon rather than from Marx that they took the project of abandoning the cities by force and re-educating the people back into agriculture. The example of Fénelon reveals why it became vital to expand the traditional canon of political thought to include religiously inspired political writers.

The problem of making a reality of communist society bedevilled 20th-century Marxists. Marx himself, having lived through the failure of the revolutions of 1848 and never seeing socialism established, was not able to provide guidance on the necessary processes for the establishment of revolution and maintenance of socialism afterwards, let alone the precise nature of the transition to communism. Those who wanted to make a success of revolutions, especially against a background of world war and ongoing civil war, had in such circumstances to look beyond Marx. This was the case especially in China after the failure of the Great Leap Forward (1958–62) to transform an agrarian economy into a hyper-productive communist society.

Marxists in government facing unrest and lacking a precise plan for social transformation generated a singular debt to Fénelon. Fénelon was famous for his learning and his Christian devotion. He was employed to teach Louis XIV's grandson, the young duke of Burgundy, who was then in line to the throne but died young. Fénelon composed a teaching manual for the duke that related the story of a young man called *Télémaque* who was led by his tutor Mentor to govern a state for the good of all of its inhabitants. *Les aventures de Télémaque, fils d'Ulysse* (*The Adventures of Telemachus, Son of Ulysses*) became the title of Fénelon's manuscript. Fénelon's guide to good rulership was at odds—indeed, it was designed entirely to condemn—the contemporary policies of Louis XIV. As such Fénelon accepted that his work would be deemed to be seditious and he sought for it to remain private.

Someone stole the manuscript of *Telemachus* and published it in 1699. It was a sensation. In due course it became the most popular secular book of the 18th century across Europe. Messages about how to govern a state were conveyed by means of the captivating story of Telemachus and his travels with Mentor in search of his father Odysseus. One of the main themes of the book was how a corrupted state addicted to the pursuit of war and the consumption of luxuries, named Salentum by Fénelon, could be turned towards more natural forms of social living. Fénelon's book was manifestly a critique of strategies for the expansion of French power in Europe by wars intended to create empires. It was also a warning of the consequences of amoral or reason-of-state policies in politics and the economy, especially when such policies were identified with the acquisition of riches by the state and by its people.

Fénelon foresaw ominous days ahead in predicting that capitalism would lead to Caesarism. Wherever commerce was advancing to the neglect of agriculture, peasants sick of poverty and attracted by promises of wealth would move to the towns and cities. In time they would lose a sense of their own identity and culture, in addition to being corrupted by loose morals and luxury. As the fortunes of trade forever oscillated the migrants would inevitably find themselves unemployed. In such circumstances, material survival would dictate enrolment as soldiers in standing armies. As armed mercenaries with no reason for devotion to a particular state, they were likely to be loyal instead to whichever general rewarded them. When and if the time came, they would follow contemporary Caesars willing to cross their own Rubicon and put an end to popular liberties where they existed. Absolute monarchy or military despotism would be the outcome.

Fénelon's solution to the problem of agricultural migrants becoming mercenaries itself required upheaval and possibly violence. Fénelon advocated taking the people from the cities by compulsion if necessary and returning them to live and to work close to the soil. Fénelon's fears and his remedies were debated throughout the 18th century. They have never gone away. Marx took much from Fénelon's critique of capitalism. He did not, however, share Fénelon's plan for the radical transformation of society.

Marxism continues to matter. In times of crisis diverse groups who see themselves to be subject to oppression can unite under the Marxist banner. In the 1960s this occurred when Marcuse, peddling an amorphous Marxism, pulled together groups demanding an end to the belittling of what was then termed 'the Third World', anti-racism and anti-capitalist activists, supporters of Black Power, exploited farmers across Africa, and Chinese Communist Party workers. The problem, as Lukács had warned in the 1920s, was that there had to be a revolutionary subject and sufficient unity not only to initiate revolution but to stabilize it on the basis of the support of a sufficiently large proportion of any society.

Chapter 4
Political philosophers and the history of political thought

Politics, philosophy, and history

If one response to Marxist approaches was that their reconstruction of historical ideas had gone astray, another was that Marxism as a philosophy was inferior to liberalism, ultimately advocating a less free and more troubled society. The view that Marxism led to Caesarism had been commonplace from the 1920s. Show trials, public confessions, and judicial murder then combined with assertions that Soviet Russia, the poster-state of Marxism, sought the overthrow of alternative political systems globally by war or revolution. Justifying a liberal philosophy underpinning a society superior in every way to Marxism became urgent with the Cold War. With post-war confidence fostered by the victory of the liberal democracies over Nazism, it appeared to many that liberal states were the future, combining freedom, welfare, and prosperity. Rational solutions to problems and faith in laws that embodied the universally defined public good characterized the times. The older empires of France and Britain fell apart. The state founded upon the renunciation of empire, the United States of America, combated communism but proclaimed no imperial mission. Its goal was rather global commerce, something that would benefit all the peoples of the earth.

Confidence in the 1950s that the 'right' system of politics, economy, and society, whether communist or capitalist, had been discovered became linked, unsurprisingly, with a turn away from history and theory. Such arguments about values and ideology were no longer necessary. Instead, science could justify social policy. Behaviouralism, propagated by Heinz Eulau, David Easton, and other political scientists, demanded the analysis of politics through the assertion of claims that could be empirically verified or refuted, making the subject explanatory and predictive on the model of the natural sciences. Every problem had a solution and the solution could always be expressed mathematically. Data analysis could test hypotheses and come up with irrefutable policy recommendations. Although trends in political science have altered, with rational choice analysis prominent and parallels emphasized with the science of economics, the rigid rejection of history has remained; if contemporary problems need to be solved, current data alone matters.

While scholars from anti-behaviourist traditions were being expelled from departments of politics and political science in many universities in the West, there was an upsurge of interest in political philosophy. Uncertainty about what a liberal society ought to look like remained a central question, especially after the anti-communist purges promoted in the United States by Senator Joseph McCarthy in the 1940s and 1950s. What liberalism meant both domestically and internationally and whether it needed to be coupled with variants of pacific socialism/communitarianism was discussed with ever more intensity after the failures of the Vietnam War, the demands of students for a more just society across the world in 1968, and accusations that the United States was not only as imperially minded as other states but erected on the racist exploitation of non-white peoples. Numerous textbooks now chart the range of post-war liberal political theory which has flourished within interdisciplinary contexts, such as the Chicago Committee on Social Thought founded in 1941 or the International Conference for the Study of Political Thought founded in 1967, because of the work of particular individuals in institutional contexts, from Leo Strauss at Chicago and Sheldon Wolin and Hannah Pitkin together at Berkeley to John Rawls, Robert Nozick, and Michael Sandel apart at Harvard.

The list of renowned political theorists turned public intellectuals has remained wide-ranging, including Norberto Bobbio, Jürgen Habermas, Julia Kristeva, and Charles Taylor; although originally an economist, Amartya Sen, should be added to the list. Yet perhaps the most notable development in political theory has been the importance of activists beyond the academy such as Jean-Paul Sartre, Simone de Beauvoir, Ayn Rand, Frantz Fanon, Julius Nyerere, Kate Millett, Malcolm X, Gustavo Gutiérrez, and Martin Luther King. All of these figures contributed to the isms found in textbooks, liberalism and neoliberalism, libertarianism, pluralism, feminism, multiculturalism, conservatism, anti-colonialism, utilitarianism, anarchism, republicanism, and communitarianism. The perspective upon the history of political thought in such diverse writing is understandably wide-ranging and cannot be covered in this short book. The most influential both in the sense of receiving philosophical commentary and the accolade that it was the most important work in political philosophy since John Stuart Mill—the parallel itself is of course telling—was that of John Rawls. Rawls is worth examining because just as his political theory transformed the field so his approach to the history of political thought has been singularly influential.

Rawls and history

Imagine that you find yourself in a seminar room at Harvard University at the beginning of the 1990s in a class being taught by the person reputed to be the greatest political philosopher of the 20th century, John Rawls (Figure 9). Rawls is revising, he says, his monumental *A Theory of Justice* (1971) in response to numerous criticisms. The book was first formulated at a time when the death of political philosophy was widely asserted. Rawls's *Theory of Justice*

9. John Rawls (1921–2002).

entirely reversed such a trend. Rawls seeks to find agreement where there is division, erecting in Kantian fashion a monument to universal justice and morality in the place of what he perceives to be the anarchies of relativism and nihilism but also the narrow justifications of law and action he associates with much contemporary utilitarian philosophy. Rawls's *Theory of Justice* defines principles justified by a hypothetical social contract derived from an original position; members of society find themselves behind a veil of ignorance preventing them from having knowledge of their abilities, class, religion, status, or place in time. Would-be citizens opt for justice as fairness, subscribing to a society in which the principle of equal liberty is enshrined, entailing freedom of thought and assembly, freedom from torture, freedom to vote and to own property. More radically, citizens behind the veil of ignorance secondarily subscribe to what Rawls called the 'difference principle', justifying inequalities alone that can be seen to maximize the wellbeing of the least well off in society. Rawls claims that his definition of personhood avoids metaphysics, that he has justified a liberalism inclusive of social welfare without being socialistic, and that his theory is of universal import.

Unsurprisingly, Rawls has been assaulted from the right for underplaying the force of self-interest and from the left for underestimating the importance of community. More generally, he wants to refute accusations that his version of Kantian moral law is North American rather than universal, being an attempt to rewrite the Constitution of the United States rather than discuss justice globally. Rawls is worried that in his work he had been too abstract, especially with regard to potential clashes between the principle of liberty and that of equality; what does it mean to create a society for the benefit of the least well off in practice? In addition to wanting to address such complaints, the later Rawls takes seriously the argument that he ignored international relations in his *Theory of Justice*.

Rawls, in presenting to students ideas that will form the basis of his next book *Political Liberalism*, which will appear in 1993, has taken the decision to engage with classic texts in the history of political thought in order to refine his theories. He hands over to his students modern editions of Hume, Rousseau, and Kant and asks you to find sections concerned with democracy. Rawls asks what you think about the arguments of each thinker? Compare them with my own, he says, and assume that we are in a dialogue with one another about the concept of democracy, what it means and how it works. You do the same with liberty, also with justice, and finally with equality.

Rawls demands that you judge for yourself the arguments of each of the historic philosophers and work out whether you should be a

Kantian, Humean, or Rousseauvian on particular questions. He is equally interested in what they would have said today about contemporary burning issues, were it possible to resurrect and engage with them. Rawls is precise in everything he says and writes. You watch him carefully refine his own argument by testing it against historic interlocutors. He is formulating a new theory of a free society, one which avoids association with a particular conception of the good life to be imposed on others, but rather which rests upon the agreement of sensible and rational individuals to the fundamental principles of a social organization, who together generate what he calls an 'overlapping consensus'. Through engagement with the great texts, the authors of which seem to have been far more ambitious than Rawls himself in their universal pronouncements, you are encouraged to contribute to the method of 'reflective equilibrium', finding a more compelling and nuanced sense of justice as fairness.

You wake up thinking that Rawls has proved that the history of political thought is directly relevant to the present. You did not have to become a Marxist to prove its utility. Then you ponder further and wonder what exactly the *history* element of the political thought was. In the authors examined, Rawls was interested in the thought not the history. Only the texts of Hume, Rousseau, and Kant mattered insofar as they were making arguments that engaged with issues in the present. Authors are read ahistorically. Any notion explicable in their own time ceases to be relevant. There is no probing of text or interest in context because you have the arguments in the published works and need nothing else. The history of the author and their time is of no consequence. Rather, Rawls is engaging with disembodied free-range philosophical claims about politics which by a series of chances happened to be published at a particular time under the authorship of particular thinkers. The portion of a text to be engaged with is equally rather small. Only assertions that are pertinent today in the sense that they can be envisaged as an ongoing conversation from past to present have any interest for his class.

You also notice that Rawls is seeking for agreement between historic thinkers with regard to what he calls public reason, the basic notions of what he calls liberalism, being the fundamental requirements for the existence of a free society. Hume, Rousseau, and Kant are interrogated about the arguments they may have formulated against freedom, in order to bolster further their own liberal theory. Rawls is following them in this practice. He is also formulating his own liberal tradition of argument, although he thinks that the existence of such a tradition merely indicates that historic philosophers have been interested in liberalism and ought to be listened to. Sense of the present being a direct product of a particular culture or historic tradition has no import for Rawls. Nor does the fact of there being a liberal tradition. The point, he says over and over again, is how coherent and sustainable arguments are from the perspective of the present.

When you explain your dream to a historian of political thought she confirms that history plays little part in Rawls's theories. She says too what you know already, that Rawls's ahistorical approach to texts is the dominant form of teaching political thought in universities across the world. It is the most straightforward because all you need to get the students to do is to open a book by a philosopher and read particular sections. It can be exciting, because you are using old books directly in the service of present politics. The 'public reason' that lies at the basis of such an approach derives from the search for arguments that are convincing and coherent. The view of Montesquieu is rejected, that general principles of liberty or anything else make no sense because what works in one place will not work in another, in part because of the force of history and culture but also because of geographical factors, such as climate, which limit political options available to a society. That Hume, Rousseau, or Kant might have themselves been adherents of Montesquieu is set aside. They are seen to be advocates of universal principles of liberty, which are deemed to exist independently of the advocacy of particular morals or cultures. That is why they are worth listening to.

Shklar and Arendt

Rawls's eminent colleague Judith Shklar, a friend and significant influence in Rawls's turn towards the writings of Hume, Rousseau, and Kant, had a different view because getting the history right mattered. Shklar argued in a series of essays and books that ahistorical theories were likely to fail in the face of cultures that rejected liberalism or whose initial assumption about liberalism was that it was an imperialist doctrine, seeking to enforce North American ways upon other societies, sustaining the dominion of this superpower while deluding itself that it was seeking to promote liberty. History was littered with tyrannies and would-be tyrants. Such societies ranged from the intolerant and oppressive to the genocidal. Yet free societies too could either easily collapse or themselves foster intolerance; too much attention was paid to the formulation of theories of justice and not enough to avoiding cruelty and injustice, the evils that Shklar claimed inspired what she termed historically 'the liberalism of fear'.

For Shklar the battle for liberty and liberalism required the formulation of tools forged through the analysis of historic texts, because cruelty and abuse were characteristic of every society ancient and modern, whatever fundamental principles or rights a society saw itself to be resting upon. Guardians of liberty were required who could tell the truth to power and identify injustice where governments refused to see it. Power needed to be spread out and balanced. It also needed to be checked repeatedly to ensure that a power once limited had not become excessive and abusive. A good example here could be found in ideas about rights, which Shklar argued were defined in the United States of America *against* other people, especially from different races, rather than being about the extent of liberty, as discussions across Europe implied.

Shklar's approach looked different from that of Rawls but in fact there were significant overlaps. The point of historical scholarship was the creation of a liberal society in the present. The object of research was texts concerned with liberty, its loss, recovery, and maintenance. Reading the main texts of canonical authors was the key to the practice of political theorizing, unless a new figure absurdly neglected proved to be espousing arguments of immediate relevance and could therefore legitimately be added to the canon. The history of political thought was perceived dialogically, being a perpetual discussion between authors putting forward different positions. It was possible, for Shklar and for Rawls, to ask what Rousseau, Montesquieu, or Hegel would have said about issues of the present. Their position could be read off from the philosophical stance they had taken in the past. Shklar's approach too proved popular. In her classes she emphasized the need for students to associate past and present. Students were expected to form their own view of the history of political thought, itself fluid and individualist, through engagement with the texts towards the goal of the education of the moderate liberal self.

Shklar believed that it was possible to read one text through another, that we cannot free ourselves from the inherited interpretative lenses through which we understand phenomena, and that philosophy is in a perpetual self-critical engagement with its own textual past. Forging concepts that helped the present understand political risk, especially the possibility of renewed descent into terror and genocide, was the point of the history of political thought. This approach was equally that of Hannah Arendt (Figure 10). Arendt had studied at Marburg between 1924 and 1929 under Martin Heidegger and wrote her dissertation in Heidelberg with Karl Jaspers, was involved with the German Zionist Organization, and escaped the Nazis, despite incarceration in internment camps in France, by emigrating to the United States. Arendt came to prominence in 1951 with her book *The Origins of Totalitarianism*.

Arendt's definition of totalitarianism was expansive. In addition to underlining the novelty of modern governmental terrorizing of the

10. Hannah Arendt (1906–75).

mass of their populations she emphasized the capacity of bureaucracies to justify victimization by reference to racial superiority and by the practice of imperial rule. Solutions were presented by Arendt to the dangers of modern politics in forms of sociability, love, and political activism in her hugely influential *The Human Condition* (1958). The book indicted western philosophy from Plato to Marx for valuing work rather than political activity. The lack of a public space for politics led to the horrors of a French Revolution dominated by issues of social structure by contrast with the American Revolution that focused instead on liberty. One message was that in modern republics liberty could so easily be lost. The function of the history of political thought was to provide general examples, such as the contrast between 18th-century revolutions, that could then be directly related to current circumstances.

Leo Strauss and Straussianism

Shklar's and Arendt's view that the history of political thought had a role to play in the shaping of character, especially as students formulated ideas for themselves through close scrutiny of classical texts, overlapped too with a more distinctive approach. Its origins were German. It was inspired by Leo Strauss and termed Straussianism. Strauss had fought for Germany in the First World War and was trained in philosophy at the University of Hamburg. His supervisor was the eminent Enlightenment scholar Ernst Cassirer. Recognizing the imperative of fleeing from the Nazis, Strauss at first went to Cambridge in the United Kingdom but then, through the help of Harold Laski and R. H. Tawney, obtained a teaching position in the United States. Becoming a US citizen in 1944, Strauss developed his approach to the history of political thought at the University of Chicago.

Strauss's book *Persecution and the Art of Writing* (1952) introduced fully to English readers notions of esoteric writing he first formulated in the late 1930s when working on Maimonides. In letters to Jacob Klein of 1938–9 Strauss exalts in the interpretative strides he is making when he recognizes that Herodotus too wrote esoterically and that there is a Plato distinct from Platonism who can be discovered by identifying the esoteric interlinkages of passages by authors addressing one another across time. Writing to Klein in November 1939 he says, 'it is beginning to dawn on me how misunderstood the ancients are'. Strauss defended writing that led the reader to ask questions for themselves, following Socrates in Plato's *Phaedrus*. The following year *Natural Right and History* (1953) appeared and quickly became a classic. Other especially influential books—Strauss wrote a very large number—were *Thoughts on Machiavelli* (1958) and *The City and Man* (1964).

Strauss had a gift for friendship. He was also very good at attracting outstanding students and influencing young scholars who had been trained by others. This facilitated his founding of a school sharing a general approach to the study of the history of political thought and philosophy. Straussians often disagreed with each other but they shared a commitment to teaching by asking questions. The asking of questions established a dialogue with students so that the students themselves commenced a revelatory intellectual journey, sometimes deemed to be more important than taking a stand on the meaning of particular historical texts. Another element of Strauss's attractiveness was undoubtedly his sense of humour, reflected in his interest in what he termed the comic equivalent, the droll way of making a serious or even a tragic point, which he found in Socrates and in Aristophanes.

Strauss believed that philosophers had three roles to play as the authors of texts. The first was to reassure existing members of society that they were living in a stable system and one likely to endure. Such messages could be conveyed by exoteric writing, explicitly supportive of the current social order. In the post-war United States, for example, philosophers writing exoterically necessarily favoured democracy and human rights. Philosophers also played a different and less obvious role. Esoteric writing was identifiable by 'reading between the lines' of a text, tantamount to working out an author's true intentions in writing. Once the reader deciphered the hidden messages in the text a more critical stance could be discerned by the original author with regard to contemporary society. This in turn established a grander and longer-term dialogue between great minds across time. The most important task of any scholar was then to decipher the esoteric meaning of a given text and its relationship with the esoteric arguments of fellow great philosophers.

The third role was educational. Philosophers laced their work with contradictions, knowing that these would shock a reader but also educate them, helping them to formulate their own views and challenge their existing opinions. The goal of reading such texts was above all the education of the mind and the enlightenment of would-be citizens. No philosophical standpoint was eternally true or likely to last. As such, creating intellectuals who recognized this and hence acquired a deep knowledge of the principles and practice of politics was vital to any society. Indeed, Strauss called such figures exponents of the 'first philosophy'.

In addition to enunciating a method for would-be philosophers rooted in the study of the history of political thought, Strauss made clear the benefits to be derived from the rediscovery of the esoteric tradition. The use of the word rediscovery is important because Strauss was certain that western societies had declined philosophically. They had lost sight of what their ancestors had achieved in erecting a critical philosophical apparatus while also hiding it from general view. The first advance was to see behind the veil of contemporary liberalism. Lovers of liberty in the ancient world had sought excellence. In modern times the aspiration to universal liberty was necessarily relativistic and risked turning nihilist. It could take the form of Nazism or Bolshevism, but it also existed in the faux egalitarian hedonism that Strauss associated with contemporary life in the United States.

Rather than understanding the modern world by reference to liberalism, Strauss taught that an altogether different perspective needed to be developed, one founded on the difference between Reason and Revelation, which he sometimes summarized by counterposing Athens to Jerusalem, perpetually struggling together with neither side ever securing an all-out victory. Strauss argued that modern philosophy had declined by defending spurious notions, such as the fact–value distinction, which gave individuals confidence about the scientific and empirical nature of judgement in contemporary societies where in fact their politics were arbitrary, misconstrued, and frequently deceptive. Analysing past texts and reconstructing alternative histories of the present made this clear, liberating students from the false assumptions about progress, science, and modern superiority.

When analysing texts with a view to recovering esoteric meanings, Strauss would look at how many times a word was used and how many chapters could be found in a work. Numerology mattered. This made reading Strauss difficult. It was clear too that he wrote esoterically, anticipating engagement with great minds both contemporary and into the future. Many of his books were summaries, following the techniques of the Islamic philosophers he had spent his early years intensively studying, such as Avicenna (Abu 'Ali al-Husayn ibn Sina, 980–1037) or Averroes (Ibn Rushd, 1126–98). In these summaries, however, Strauss might leave something out or reconstruct a passage in a distinctive manner or make a comment that the reader was expected to explore and develop themselves.

An example is a note in his *Thoughts on Machiavelli* (1958) which the leading Straussian Harvey C. Mansfield deciphered while working on Machiavelli himself and using Strauss's book as his guide. According to Mansfield, what Strauss left unsaid but could be deciphered by the esoteric clues left in his text was that if Machiavelli's two books, *The Prince* and the *Discourses on Livy*, are considered together there are 14 uses of the term 'form' and 51 uses of the word 'matter'. Initiates would recognize that such terms signified engagement with the debate about nature (*physis*) and convention, law, or custom (*nomos*) in ancient philosophy. The number 14 was a multiple of 7 and the number 7 signified *nomos*. The number 51 was a multiple of 17, and the number 17 in turn signified *physis*.

Such numbers revealed that Machiavelli was taking a stand by arguing against *physis*, that there were no real essences in politics and that fortune could be tamed by humans taking control of their own destiny. That this was Machiavelli's own voice arguing intentionally was evident from the fact that if the number of appearances of the terms for *nomos* and *physis* were added together they totalled 65, a division of 13, which was the author's own number in the sense that he was signalling that his own views *were* being presented in the text. Such evidence pointed, according to Mansfield, to the need to treat *The Prince* and the *Discourses* together as one book conveying related arguments and sharing an intellectual mission.

Machiavelli's mission according to Strauss was human mastery over fortune, the random force that could be tamed by the bending of nature to human will. The turn away from nature as a philosophical subject was continued by Francis Bacon and Thomas Hobbes, all moderns together with John Locke, whose praise of labour to control nature as a key to human fulfilment equally marked the intellectual turn. Strauss worried that the denial of nature led to relativism and that in rejecting natural foundations for any human belief the origins of the horror of 20th-century war could be found. A rebalancing of philosophy was therefore necessary. Such goals, however lofty they might seem, were to be realized by returning to Socratic questions, asking what something was and what functions it served. Strauss called for a return to the ancients in the hope of challenging contemporary liberal platitudes, which he perceived to be dangerously arrogant, arguing instead in favour of a variety of ways of living, some of which might well eschew the active life controlling nature so venerated by moderns.

Strauss reinterpreted figures major and minor in the history of political thought. Moderns had turned away from the wisdom especially of the ancients with regard to the nature of the good life. There was no single truth to be conveyed about politics—this was why the modern social sciences had gone astray—but rather a process of seeking truth which led to political moderation and knowledge. The power and appeal of Strauss can be seen in the prominence and variety of his followers. These have been numerous, divided East Coast and West Coast, and distinguished, from historians of political thought such as Harry V. Jaffa, Steven B. Smith, and Thomas M. Pangle to card carrying philosophers such as Stanley Rosen or Heinrich Meier to leading cultural critics such as Allan Bloom.

Chapter 5
The 'Cambridge School'

The origins of the study of political thought in Britain

The so-called Cambridge School of the History of Political Thought has been the most influential among scholars. It rejected Marxist approaches for propagating bad history. Almost every element of the story of the Cambridge School can be contested, including, as the use of the term 'so-called' implies, its title. The reason for the complexity of the story is that the Cambridge School is accepted as being the product of the labours of three scholars with divergent interests and careers, John Pocock, Quentin Skinner, and John Dunn, all of whom formulated their ideas about how the history of political thought should become a field with a method separately and together in the 1960s. The term 'Cambridge School' derives from the fact that all three were associated with the University of Cambridge. Understanding what they found and why they wanted to do things differently requires a short reconstruction of the history of political thought in Britain in general and Cambridge in particular. The story is tied to the history of liberalism, meaning the story of Britain as a prominent liberal state.

Most liberals—those who began to use the word to describe themselves in the early 19th century—thought that a reformed version of the British constitution operating in different forms of society would maintain order and liberty. Ideally this would be achieved without recourse to the kinds of Christian fanaticism characteristic of the Holy Alliance between Austria, Prussia, and Russia or indeed the civil violence that had marred the French Revolution. Prominent liberals, such as Anne-Louise Germaine de Staël, Benjamin Constant, or Simonde de Sismondi, were all obsessed by the lessons of historical forms of politics for the present. Speculation about avoiding corruption, nationalism, and mercantile imperialism became central to liberal philosophy, while retaining the social hierarchies sufficient to retain order and ensure economic development. Britain without Britishness was one popular definition of liberalism.

At the same time the French Revolution led to the creation of new human sciences. Many radicals who had initially been swayed by the fervour for liberty turned to educational schemes to teach moderation and the avoidance of conflict. Others, such as the poets Samuel Taylor Coleridge and William Wordsworth, moved against having any direct role for the people in government. Jeremy Bentham, who blamed Britain's mercantile system for rejecting his panopticon prison intended to 'grind rogues honest', became convinced that a science of political tactics needed to be constructed. It would teach would-be legislators and politicians how to enact the utilitarian laws that embodied the public good of the greatest number. It would also ensure that such laws were adhered to.

The early 19th century was an age of projects. Liberty and prosperity were the goals of statesmen so long as the worst excesses of revolution were prevented from returning. A new focus upon the education of broader populations led both to the opening up of the universities and the creation of new subjects. At different times and in different places the history of political thought became an independent subject. At the same time, there was a movement away from history in some of the newly demarcated research fields, because history was presented as the less certain and less objective component of human science. The most important instance was political economy.

Numerous political economists, such as David Ricardo, for a variety of reasons amputated Smith's historical grounding of the subject. Ricardo was a philosophical radical and close to Bentham. It is sometimes claimed that Benthamite utilitarianism rejected history because adherents like Ricardo or jurists such as John Austin wanted to model the new science on geometry. Other followers of Bentham, from George Grote to John Roebuck, were wedded to history as the basis of the study of politics. Bentham's most important disciple, James Mill, sought compromise between the historical and the geometrical. Tension was the result. Political science was defined as resting upon demonstrative facts, having first principles and self-evident truths axiomatic in their nature. Alternatively, it was a storehouse of evaluative and comparative knowledge, a philosophy capable of directing present politics through the scrutiny of historic examples. Opposition between these approaches still marks the study of politics in our own time.

If university lectures dealing with the history of political ideas as a branch of the science of politics abounded as the 19th century progressed, increasingly they were published as books. One in particular was influential across Europe, Johann Caspar Bluntschli's three-volume *Theory of the State* (*Lehre vom modernen Stat*), the product of lectures at the universities of Munich and Heidelberg. Bluntschli had been a student of Friedrich Carl von Savigny at Berlin. Savigny, the brilliant historian of Roman Law, argued against attempts to universalize law in the manner of the Code Napoléon or proposals for unified legal codes across Germany. For Savigny, law had to reflect national spirit (*Volksgeist*), being adapted to historical understandings of law in particular communities. Politics too should not be axiomatic because of the gulf between the specification of a right embodied by law and the way that it would be interpreted in accordance with local historical practice. Bluntschli shared Savigny's view. As a Swiss liberal republican, he sought in his *Theory of the State* to work out why the 1848 revolutions had not established a liberal Europe. Equally, he examined the strategies alternative to revolution that might result in creating a state governed in accordance with civil liberties and the rule of law (*Rechtsstaat*).

Bluntschli's book became a textbook for courses in political philosophy, jurisprudence, and the science of politics. From the 1870s, for example, it was used at the University of Cambridge in the compulsory course Principles of Political Philosophy and General Jurisprudence, in the 1880s for the compulsory course Political Science, in the 1890s for the course Comparative Politics, in the 1910s Political Science. These courses were forerunners of those established in the 1930s with the titles The History of Political Thought and The Theory of the Modern State (from 1951 Theories of the Modern State).

In the story of the establishment of the study of the history of political thought as a branch of political science at the University of Cambridge, Whigs and Liberals played a major role. In the forefront was Robert Seeley (1834–95), Regius Professor of Modern History from 1869 until his death. Seeley was the author of *The Expansion of England* (1883), a defence of a liberal conception of empire as improvement. Seeley's view of the direct link between history and present politics meant that in the 1880s students who took the course Political Science, for example, would read Bluntschli, Henry James Sumner Maine's *Ancient Law: Its Connection with the Early History of Society and its Relation to Modern Ideas*, first published in 1861, Herbert Spencer's *Political Institutions, being Part V of the Principles of Sociology* of 1882, George Grote's *History of Greece* published from 1846, and Theodor Mommsen's *History of Rome*, which appeared from 1854.

By the 1910s students taking Political Science would read a book by another major liberal figure, Henry Sidgwick's *Development of the European Polity*, in addition to primary texts by Aristotle, Hobbes, and more modern works by James Mill, T. H. Green, and Bernard Bosanquet (*The Philosophical Theory of the State*, 1899). Works devoted to the history of political thought specifically began to appear. In 1901 John Neville Figgis published *Political Thought from Gerson to Grotius*. The advocate of church councils Jean Gerson (1363–1429), sometime chancellor of the University of Paris, was praised by Figgis as a foundational figure in the history of constitutionalism. Ernest Barker followed with *The Political Thought of Plato and Aristotle* in 1906 and *Political Thought in England from Herbert Spencer to the Present Day* in 1915. In the same year H. W. C. Davies published *The Political Thought of Heinrich Von Treitschke*. In 1920 Barker's student Harold Laski published *Political Thought in England from Locke to Bentham*. The subject was by now a staple of academic research and teaching. There was a battle from the left and the right of the political spectrum to make the subject their own.

Studying the history of political thought at Cambridge

At Cambridge after the Second World War the field of the history of political thought became still more prominent. Walter Ullmann lectured on medieval political thought, having published *Medieval Papalism: The Political Theories of the Medieval Canonists* in 1949. D. W. Brogan, as Professor of Political Science from 1939, focused on the history of ideas in France and the contemporary United States of America. Duncan Forbes from 1947 also taught modern political thought. Forbes was distinctive in paying attention to Hegel and 19th-century German intellectual history. He was equally innovative in creating a special subject for final-year students in the early 1960s devoted to the Scottish Enlightenment. This course was taken by Quentin Skinner, John Dunn, and Nicholas Phillipson as undergraduates.

The most influential figure at Cambridge was, however, Peter Laslett. At the end of the 1940s Laslett published an edition of Robert Filmer's work as *Patriarcha and Other Political Writings*. He went on to study the diverse idiomatic responses to Filmer by John Locke, Algernon Sidney, William Petyt, Henry Neville, and others, resulting in his seminal edition of Locke's *Two Treatises* in 1960. Laslett provided solid proof that if you investigated the publishing history of a text and an author's intentions then the meaning of the text could be reconstructed. Laslett revealed that Filmer's *Patriarcha* had been composed prior to his other writings but published posthumously between 1679 and 1680. Locke's classic work of political thought, rather than being a defence of the 'Glorious Revolution', as it had traditionally been described, having appeared in print from 1689 (although it says 1690 on the title page), was shown to have been written around 1681, at a time when Whigs of Locke's stamp were contemplating violence against the Stuart court. Laslett revealed what has been called the mystery of contextualization.

It is significant that Laslett, who had done so much to promote new approaches to the history of political thought, then abandoned the subject. As early as 1958 Laslett had complained about teaching in Cambridge. He observed that the History of Political Thought and Theories of the Modern State courses taught undergraduates that 'Plato, Aristotle, Aquinas, Hobbes, Locke, Rousseau, Burke, Marx and all the other Really Big Names felt that empirical and theoretical study of society was of the foremost importance'. Yet the undergraduates were not then taught themselves to move from past to present. In other words, they did not study their own society in the same way that such giants in the history of political thought had studied their own, by empirical and theoretical analysis. Cambridge, Laslett complained, had 'no teachers of politics, no sociology, and the smallest number of philosophers, in relation to our size, in the whole wide world'.

Laslett himself soon moved into other fields. Initially he was attracted by the verification principle associated with the philosophical school known as Logical Positivism, but also the falsification principle associated with Popper and his acolytes. He then investigated social structures through the techniques of historical demography. He was ultimately convinced that it was better to rely on the social sciences if you wanted to understand the past. In Laslett's view, such a linkage made the relevance of historical enquiry to solving contemporary social issues much more obvious. Laslett remained an innovator. He co-founded the Cambridge Group for the History of Population and Social Structure in 1964, the Open University in 1965, and the University of the Third Age in 1981.

While Laslett was researching when and why texts had been published R. G. Collingwood's posthumously published *The Idea of History* (1946) recommended distinguishing between the 'outside' of events, facts about moving bodies, and the 'inside' of an action, why a person did what they did by reference to the ideas in their mind. Julius Caesar's assassination, for example, could only ultimately be explained through perceptions of Caesar as a tyrant subverting the liberties of the Roman people and therefore the existence of the Roman Republic. At the same time as Collingwood's book was becoming influential Michael Oakeshott gave his inaugural lecture of 1951 at the London School of Economics with the title 'Political Education'. Here Oakeshott referred to 'tradition' as a flexible inheritance every person defined themselves by reference to. He justified historical analysis of past and present political ideas as a means of practical benefit, to be contrasted with the arid scrutiny of doctrines and systems.

The identity of the Cambridge School

All three founders of the Cambridge School were inspired by Laslett's reconstruction of the historical context of Locke's and Filmer's books which then transformed their meaning. Pocock was the oldest, being born in London in 1924 and emigrating to New Zealand as a young child when his father, Greville Agard Pocock, became Professor of Classics at Canterbury College. Pocock graduated from Canterbury himself then moved to Cambridge in 1948, completing a Ph.D. under Herbert Butterfield in 1952. Following teaching posts at Otago, at St John's College, Cambridge, and at Canterbury, Pocock in 1966 became the William Eliot Smith Professor of History at Washington University in St. Louis. In the mid-1970s he moved to a chair at Johns Hopkins University in Baltimore. By 1957 he was well known because of his first book *The Ancient Constitution and the Feudal Law*. In 1975 the book that is sometimes seen as a classic statement of the Cambridge approach, *The Machiavellian Moment*, appeared. Such works were followed by further prominent books and a vast body of essays, up to the six-volume *Barbarism and Religion* studies of the intellectual world of Edward Gibbon and his *History of the Decline and Fall of the Roman Empire*.

Quentin Skinner was born in 1940, took an undergraduate degree at Cambridge, and was appointed to a lectureship in the Faculty of History in 1965. From this time his writings on the proper method of study for the history of political thought were bringing him to attention, in addition to a series of iconoclastic essays on Hobbes published in *The Historical Journal* and in *Comparative Studies in Society and History*. After a period spent at Princeton University's Institute for Advanced Study in the 1970s, Skinner became Professor of Political Science at Cambridge in 1978 and Regius Professor of History in 1996 before moving to Queen Mary, University of London, in 2008. Skinner's *The Foundations of Modern Political Thought* was published in two volumes in 1978 and has become the most widely cited and commented-upon book in the field. Skinner followed it with pathbreaking essays and books on a large number of subjects, from ancient Roman notions of rhetoric and morality to the formation of the Italian city republics and Machiavelli, to Renaissance rhetoric and Hobbes and Shakespeare, to the nature of liberty ancient, early modern, and contemporary. Due to these works, abetted by brilliance as a lecturer and writer, Skinner continues to personify the history of political thought as a subject.

At Cambridge in the early 1960s John Dunn and Quentin Skinner were undergraduates together and close friends. Their first intellectual labours were similarly shared. Dunn's book *The Political Thought of John Locke: An Historical Account of the Argument of the 'Two Treatises of Government'* of 1969 epitomized the Cambridge School approach to the history of political thought as it was then defining itself. Dunn transformed understanding of Locke by showing that, rather than being a founder of modern liberalism, he was a product of radical Calvinist politics. The religious context of the second half of the 17th century best explained what Locke saw himself to have been doing. Dunn, like Skinner, was appointed to a lectureship in Cambridge, rose to become Professor of Political Theory in 1987, and became a leading historically minded political theorist. Dunn's major books include *Western Political Theory in the Face of the Future* (1979), *The History of Political Theory and Other Essays* (1996), *The Cunning of Unreason* (2000), *Setting the People Free* (2005), and *Breaking Democracy's Spell* (2014), all of which give a sense of how the history of political thought can be used to address urgent issues in contemporary societies.

What is the Cambridge method? In 1962 Pocock published the essay 'The History of Political Thought: A Methodological Enquiry'. Historic authors, Pocock argued, were members of communities using languages or discourses formed not only by rules of grammar but by inherited conventions about ideas. Discourses of ideas formed an ideological context or paradigm through which an author could express their thoughts. Discourses limited political options. In articulating their ideas authors might alter paradigms either consciously or unconsciously. Reference to a 'paradigm' underlined the influence of Thomas Kuhn's *The Structure of Scientific Revolutions* (1962) in which 'paradigm shift' occurred within a scientific community when the 'normal science' of accepted beliefs changed to another set of beliefs held to be more reflective of objective reality. Paradigms in politics for Pocock were less connected to science or progress but nevertheless imposed particular ways of thinking upon historical actors who might then transform them.

Pocock's speculations were more precisely articulated after the appearance of John Dunn's 'The Identity of the History of Ideas' in 1968 and Quentin Skinner's 'The Limits of Historical Explanations' in 1966 and 'Meaning and Understanding in the History of Ideas' in 1969. Pocock, Skinner, and Dunn shared the goal of revealing what an author of a particular text was doing in writing a text and explaining how a writer's intentions were received and modified by other authors engaging with an original text. One of the central consequences of the approach was to broaden the study of political thought beyond the presumed canonical texts; the original title of Skinner's 'Meaning and Understanding' was 'The Unimportance of the Great Texts in the History of Political Thought'. Broadening the canon and moving beyond the study of the texts of 'great' men remained one of Skinner's central goals. When he published his *The Foundations of Modern Political Thought* it was striking that no author's name appeared in any of the chapter titles.

Discontinuity in the history of political ideas was emphasized by Pocock, Skinner, and Dunn. Against Leo Strauss, they did not believe that philosophers throughout history addressed the same questions. There was no such thing as 'dateless wisdom'. Equally, texts could never be understood if they were treated as stand-alone documents whose meaning could easily be discerned by the act of philosophical reading, whose meaning was forever shifting as the French post-structuralists held, or whose content was determined by the social and economic context of the text's production. Skinner was especially effective in attacking historians of political thought who attributed to past authors concepts that could never have existed in their world; one such was the prominent founder of the History of Ideas Club, A. O. Lovejoy, who advocated the analysis of 'unit ideas' over long periods of time.

Such approaches Skinner condemned for being anachronistic. Historians of political thought who found in earlier texts anticipations of arguments of later provenance committed another sin, that of prolepsis. For Skinner textual arguments amounted to acts performed in history against a background of contextual confirmatory and refutatory assertions in related or opposed texts. The objective of the historian of political thought was to reveal what the author of a particular text 'was doing', encompassing what the author had intended to do and had succeeded in doing as interpreted by the responses of other authors. Language or discourse set limits to the potential range of political assertions.

The consequences of the Cambridge School

The sense of joint endeavour and alliance between Pocock, Skinner, and Dunn was fostered by the sharing of new work and communication about the state of the field of the history of political thought. In the 1970s Pocock contemplated writing a book on method to be entitled 'The Cave of Speech' or 'How to do Things to People with Words'. At one point it was to be a joint manifesto with Skinner concerned with 'How to Do Things to People with Words and How to Respond to People's Attempts to Do Things to You'. Yet there were differences from the first between Pocock, Skinner, and Dunn in part because of the diverse influences upon them.

Skinner and Dunn were indebted to John Austin's *How to Do Things with Words* (1962) and Oxford language philosophy more generally while Pocock emphasized a debt to Michael Oakeshott's sense of language and tradition. In the 1970s Skinner reformulated his view of the history of political thought in a further body of articles formulated in part during an extended sabbatical at Princeton. John Dunn from the early 1970s shifted his interests towards the study of revolution across Africa and its consequences for political theory. Pocock developed his long-standing interests in historiography as a form of political thought until this became the focus of his work. Skinner increasingly worried about accusations, of which he bore the brunt, that he was responsible for turning the history of political thought into an antiquarian subject, irrelevant and comprised largely of navel-gazing.

In response it could be said that the Cambridge School established what amounted to a new subject methodologically, inspired the next generation of scholars to broaden remarkably the traditional authorial canon, and provided a far more sophisticated and nuanced sense of what historical politics meant. The history of political thought countered the prevalent assumption that the past is inferior to the present and simpler to understand than the contemporary world. In the hands of Pocock, Skinner, and Dunn the history of political thought became necessary knowledge, vital for any reflective politics or informed political judgement—the kinds of judgement in increasing short supply in a world led by the advertising industry, as Adorno and Horkheimer had foreseen. Equally, the history of political thought could be conceived of as an essential element of civic education, although again this was not being realized in practice.

The achievement of the Cambridge School becomes clear when Whiggish approaches to the past are examined. If the eminent academic and Liberal politician H. A. L. Fisher's *The Republican Tradition in Europe* (1911) is compared with Pocock and Skinner it reads as literature for children. Focus upon the recovery of neglected or lost historical traditions of argument has become the defining feature of the School. Pocock and Skinner in the 1970s refined the work of Hans Baron in restoring to view a perspective upon human flourishing formulated in the Italian city republics of the early Renaissance. A life lived as a leader of a household in an independent republic was praised as natural to man. Civic activity by the cultivation of land, the practice of arms, and the making of laws to sustain this state became the highest secular aspiration. Pocock's *The Machiavellian Moment* of 1975 revealed what happened to civic humanists in time of crisis, when they were forced to use their knowledge of the virtues fostered through civic action to try to maintain their state and their sense of liberty.

Pocock detailed the intense controversy in 18th-century Europe and North America over the loss of civic virtue and the manliness that sustained it, in the very different context of urban societies and competing commercial monarchies. This approach was a world away from Marxist focus upon class antagonisms and the search for evidence of class consciousness in preparation for the revolutionary move to the next stage of history. It equally rejected reconstructions of a liberal canon, the search in the past for figures who most closely approximated those deemed worthy in the present, underscored by their support for the independence of the North American colonies within the British Empire. Pocock instead charted the controversy as to whether maintaining commercial monarchies with rapacious appetites for expanding their markets necessitated the development of standing armies and public credit.

Permanent mercenary armies sustained by public borrowing were defended by Daniel Defoe and Bernard Mandeville because of the benefits they were seen to bring, modern forms of politeness, consumption, wealth, and financial independence. 'Neo-Harringtonians', as Pocock termed them, such as the Scottish critic of the union of 1707 Andrew Fletcher of Saltoun, favoured ancient prudence, reliance upon independent landed proprietors. Such men, inspired by their love of virtue and of country, formed an elite of landowners serving when necessary in defensive militias, whose interest in the state ensured their wisdom and the moderation of their laws.

The neo-Harringtonians despised modern politeness, believing it to entail the corrosion of masculinity, the growth of forms of corruption accompanying the rise of parties and the specialist politician, and far greater uncertainty in civil society and in politics, exemplified by the reliance of the state upon the expertise of the stock-jobber. One of Pocock's most forceful points was that such views, a critique of capitalism long before Marx, could be discerned in subsequent political argument, especially in the United States with its obsessions with militias, masculinity, and the right to bear arms. Those who instead saw the birth of the United States as a glorious story of liberals establishing forms of liberty that could then be perfected over time, such as Joyce Appleby, were furious.

If Pocock worried about the diversification of the human personality in commercial society and the loss of independence, Skinner's focus became the loss of liberty. In *Liberty before Liberalism* (1998) Skinner recovered a buried tradition of political argument that had manifested itself after the regicide of the English monarch Charles I in 1649. John Milton and Marchamont Nedham, apologists for the new English Republic, asserted that the actions of a political body had to be determined by the will of its members. Advocating representation rather than democracy, they defined democracy as a system in which the people acted as their own government. Representation, by contrast, was one means of promoting government by the most virtuous and most wise; to this end Milton and Nedham recognized that it would also be vital to have laws that encouraged manliness (*virtù*) in the people, raising the possibility of laws to force citizens to be free.

Arguing against the exercise of prerogative power by governments, Milton and Nedham held that the existence of such executive powers rendered subjects or citizens unfree because of the threat to life and to property inherent in the existence of such powers. As such, they countered Hobbes's definition of a free man as someone 'not hindered to do what he has a will to'. Skinner has termed the doctrine of Milton, Nedham, and their associates 'the neo-roman theory of free states and free citizens' because they derived so much of their praise for civil liberty and political action from Cicero, Sallust, Seneca, and Tacitus.

In his *Oceana* of 1656 James Harrington responded to Hobbes's famous critique of republican liberty that the freedom proclaimed on the turrets of Lucca was illusory because the lives of the citizens of the city-state could be interfered with by their magistrates in the same way as the Ottoman sultan did with his own subjects. Harrington's reply was that 'even the greatest bashaw in Constantinople is merely a tenant of his head' because the sultan could execute a person at will. Skinner concluded that this illustrated Harrington's neo-Roman obsession with certain civil rights to be asserted against governmental power. That someone is not free unless they are free from direct coercion, or indeed from the threat or likelihood of coercion, is a perspective that Skinner wants to reassert today, especially in cases where we may presume ourselves to be free, but where we are not because of the coercive potential of state action, or that of other corporate bodies.

This meant that Skinner has been formulating a perspective on the contemporary failure to recognize the limits upon our liberty akin to that of Foucault. Skinner condemns contemporary capitalist societies characterized by mass communication and governmental and corporate observation of citizens, the scrutiny of private life, and the manipulation of desires to foster ever-greater spending on consumer products. In Skinner's view, we think we are free but in fact are slaves. To restore a sense of our loss of liberty and the dangers it poses to us, we need to go back to the neo-Romans of the 17th century who faced a related predicament.

If Skinner's work in charting the history of liberty and the identity of slavery resonates with present issues, Pocock's emphasis upon the importance of historiography in political thought merits attention. Pocock had long been fascinated by Maori perceptions of the past and their response to the Treaty of Waitangi of 1840. The Treaty was signed by more than 500 Maori leaders, including a number of women chiefs, intending to retain ownership of their land and acquire rights as British subjects while ceding sovereignty to Britain. Violations of the Treaty led to war and grotesque abuses of the Maori people. Reflection upon the history of New Zealand led Pocock in a lecture in 1973 to call for a 'new British history' bringing indigenous and migrant peoples together as *tangata waka* (peoples of the ship) who shared islands and discoveries but often differed in their sense of community, language, and history. Alternative stories then shared created conversations. These Pocock believed could ensure that moderates addressed contested political questions, including political sovereignty in New Zealand/Aotearoa and the redress of long-standing Maori grievances.

For Pocock no history was ever final. National histories ought never to define a closed world; they had to be about interactions with outsiders who might themselves become members of an altered national community. In envisaging 'histories which empower Others to act upon one while one acts upon them', facilitating political conversation and peace became part of a vision in which history shapes identity and multiple identities frame lives accepting of and comprising rival narratives.

The transformation of the history of political thought

Although there is now a minor industry in commentary upon and criticism of the Cambridge School, there can be no doubt that we are in an infinitely better position to understand the history of political thought than we were in the 1960s. One reason is because of the emphasis of Skinner and Pocock especially, following Laslett, upon the production of scholarly editions of texts that provide readers with original editions, variants, and contextual information about the writing and publication of the work. Some of the editions can be described as monumental, such as Noel Malcolm's *Leviathan: The English and Latin Texts* (2014), Knud Haakonssen's and Paul Wood's Edinburgh Edition of the Works of Thomas Reid, or Philip Schofield's editions of Bentham's writings under the auspices of The Bentham Project. In addition to such classics, popular editions are more accessible than ever before with series such as the Cambridge Texts in the History of Political Thought, which now has over a hundred titles, and the Natural Law and Enlightenment Classics published by Liberty Fund.

Editions of correspondence are now legion and access to published editions of texts is possible either directly through online searches or through digital libraries. Scholarship in the history of political thought is more extensive than ever before and more popular with publishers. Most publishers have series in political thought following Cambridge's Ideas in Context model and the range and depth of scholarship is evident by examining monographs. If work on any figure then deemed major or minor in the history of political thought is scrutinized via books published in the 1950s or 1960s and then compared with those that have appeared in subsequent decades a sense of a paradigm shift in knowledge is apparent. Scholarship, anthologies, and editions concerned with race and identity are now appearing, such as *Black Political Thought from David Walker to the Present* (2019).

Chapter 6
Koselleck and conceptual history

The German catastrophe

How could the state famous for the study of the history of political thought in the guise of *Ideengeschichte* (history of ideas) or *Geistesgeschichte* (history of the mind or spirit), the identification of the 'spirit' of an age and its manifestation in politics, expounded by such eminent scholars such as Wilhelm Dilthey (1833–1911), Ernst Cassirer (1874–1945), and Friedrich Meinecke (1862–1964), end up as the site of the Third Reich and the Holocaust? What had gone wrong with the deeper German traditions of philology and lexicography, associated especially with studies of the classical past in the 19th century but also with such projects as Jakob Grimm's and Wilhelm Grimm's vast *Deutsches Wörterbuch* (*German Dictionary*) initiated in 1838? In such scholarship, systematic knowledge (*Wissenschaft*) had been pursued through the definition of foundational concepts followed by the use of casuistic techniques to examine particular or problematic cases. From a post-war perspective, however rich the historical scholarship of the past, there had been, as Meinecke put it in 1946, an ideological disaster. He termed it *The German Catastrophe* (*Die deutsche Katastrophe*).

A major problem for writers such as Meinecke was that even a decade earlier their perspective upon past and present had been very different. In 1936 Meinecke had published *Die Enstehung des Historismus* (translated as *Historism* in 1972), a more positive evaluation of historical scholarship in Germany. Meinecke praised the German rejection of the French Revolution and secular justifications of progress in favour of the study of the particular cultures of nations, facilitating the development of healthy patriotic cultures and communities. The latter approach had been founded by Johann Gottfried Herder (1744–1803) and J. W. von Goethe (1749–1832) and exemplified by the scholarship of Leopold von Ranke (1795–1886). In 1946 Meinecke altered his perspective, blaming Ranke for praising Bismarck. Meinecke venerated instead the Swiss-German historian Jacob Burckhardt (1818–97), writing in the second half of the 19th century, for warning the German people against excessive love for war, Caesar figures, and nationalism. Burckhardt's had been a siren voice. Meinecke could not explain why he had not been listened to.

The foundations of *Begriffsgeschichte*

How then to explain the disaster of modern history and the failure of historical sensibility in Germany? New techniques to investigate the past were considered necessary to explain both German history and the sense of national and cultural failure. The project of *Begriffsgeschichte* or 'conceptual history' was a leading response, first formulated in the 1950s by the historians Otto Brunner, Werner Conze, and Reinhart Koselleck; a journal entitled the *Archiv für Begriffsgeschichte* was published from 1955. Conze was a prominent social historian based at Heidelberg. Brunner was at the time the best known, having authored a series of pathbreaking studies of medieval politics, landownership, and feudal rule, *Land und Herrschaft* (1939), *Adeliges Landleben und europäischer Geist* (1949), and later the *Neue Wege der Sozialgeschichte* (1956).

Land und Herrschaft, which Brunner revised in 1941, 1943, and 1959, asserted that it was a mistake to apply to the Middle Ages the state/civil society distinction formulated in the 18th century. Modern notions of states in medieval times exercising powers of law, war, and taxation had to be rejected. Rather, communities had been formed around ideas about transcendent justice or sacred right to which all persons were subject. Powerful notions of justice derived from perspectives upon the health of the family and the household had predominated until commerce corroded feudal social forms. Brunner's work could easily be fitted into narratives rejecting liberalism and democracy in favour of the special communal forces evident in the history of the German people (*Volksgeschichte*). For a time, Brunner had supported National Socialism as a means of challenging the selfish individualism of bourgeois societies. After the war, his critique of the liberal/constitutional state (*Rechtsstaat*) could equally be applied to the horrors of the Third Reich. As such, Brunner provided evidence that false history led to monstrous politics. What was required was a more particular understanding of what went wrong long after the collapse of the medieval community, turning those like Brunner who were critical of liberalism into scholars who, even for a time, accepted the logic of dictatorship, the abandonment of civil and political liberties, and the hounding to death of groups considered enemies of the true community of German souls.

The leader of the project from the first was Koselleck (1923–2006). After joining the Hitler Youth and serving in the Germany army towards the end of the Second World War, Koselleck was captured by Soviet troops and taken to Auschwitz to work on dismantling the instruments of mass murder. He was then held as a prisoner of war in Kazakhstan until 1946, being allowed to return home because of war wounds. These experiences shaped Koselleck's perspective upon the past, especially his acute scepticism of ideologies that purported to offer easy solutions to problems and his sense of history as a story of ceaseless conflict.

A major influence upon Koselleck was the sometime Catholic jurist Carl Schmitt (1888–1985), the arch-critic of Weimar parliamentary government as institutionalized division and of liberal-democratic society as mass chaos. Schmitt had defined politics as struggle and the sovereign in a state as the authority defining friends and enemies, vital in times of crisis when exceptional steps might need to be taken by a dictatorial executive to maintain the rule of law. Although Schmitt saw himself to be a critic of both Nazi and communist subverters of law, recognizing that liberalism and democracy had failed and that the state needed to prevent a descent into anarchy, he joined the Nazi Party in 1933 and was vocal in both his anti-Semitism and support for Hitler. What Koselleck appreciated, like so many figures subsequently influenced by Schmitt on the left and right of politics, was a focus upon ingrained conflict in modern societies and the difficulty of bringing ideologically opposed parties, themselves akin to fanatic religious groups, to a state of peace.

In the late 1950s Koselleck suggested to Conze the notion of a one-volume dictionary of historical concepts. Conze limited the project to the German language and organized contributors and funding. The goal of the project was to chart political and social change by monitoring the use of concepts, the manner by which authors in a particular period defined themselves and used language, changing the meaning of particular words or modifying their functions during the practical and ideological political battles they fought. The meaning of democracy, for example, changed from ancient times, where it was associated with the direct rule of the citizenry potentially selected for office by lot, to modern, where it might be associated with the rise of Caesar figures or descents into anarchy and terror. Working out what politics was about meant clarifying thought over time, as reflected by the meaning of words enunciated in the form of struggling concepts adapting themselves to new circumstances.

The project culminated in the multivolume lexicon or *Geschichtliche Grundbegriffe* of more than 130 concepts perceived to be of fundamental importance in society that appeared between 1972 and 1997. The lexicon aimed at registering conceptually the demise of feudal society and the emergence of the modern world. The presumption was that wide-ranging structural changes took place after 1750 that drastically changed the social, political, and economic world of estates and the manner in which contemporaries understood their experience of politics and life. Central concepts whose meaning changed, such as 'liberty' or 'people', Koselleck himself explained in the more than a hundred entries he authored, both revealed that structural change had occurred and that concepts facilitated historical change. Concepts that had been specific became universal and abstract. More people participated in political discourse, so that the usage of central concepts could be said to have been democratized (*Demokratisierung*). Concepts that had been general, such as democracy itself, gradually began to be perceived as part of a project for political change and improvement into the future (*Verzeitlichung*). The association of individual concepts with reform programmes facilitated their incorporation into economic and social ideologies (*Ideologisierbarkeit*). Politicization occurred (*Politisierung*) when concepts were used to engage and mobilize people from an increasingly broad social background during conflicts about forms of government, social structures, and the future of society.

Koselleck's view of modern thought

For all of the contributors to the *Geschichtliche Grundbegriffe* there was a sense of nostalgia for the pre-modern past and a sense of the limitations of modern ideologies, especially in their tendency to generate political extremism. It was, however, in Koselleck's hands alone that such sentiments were translated into an approach to history in general and the history of political thought in particular. Koselleck was trained at and then taught at the University of Heidelberg, where he was influenced by the philosopher Karl Löwith's view of modern ideologies, forms of modern philosophies that were ultimately secularized theology, prophecies promising the salvation of the portions of humanity who had faith in their doctrine.

In 1954 Koselleck published *Kritik und Krise* (*Critique and Crisis*). This influential book argued that the absolutist state of early modern Europe, justified by the work of philosophers such as Thomas Hobbes, had successfully put an end to the wars of religion by limiting the relationship between morality and politics. Politics was a sphere of obedience and judgement seeking peace at all costs, allowing private life to thrive but preventing moral consciences from taking over the political realm. During the Enlightenment, however, private clubs and societies, from philosophic salons to masonic lodges and the secretive gatherings of the Illuminati, had thrived, themselves a product of the circumstances of relative societal stability and peace. These groups shared the view that the state lacked moral legitimacy in failing to develop forms of civil society supportive of the strong forms of sociability and community life associated with general human happiness, wellbeing, and morality. In short, the state was not doing enough for the personal development of subjects or citizens and needed to foster their happiness as well as their security. Humanity deserved more, and contemporary states in the 18th century were derided for failing to meet the deeper needs of their peoples.

Koselleck argued that such attacks on Enlightenment states were utopian, having no sense of the realities of power politics and presenting no genuine alternative definition of a state. Equally, the Enlightenment attacks on the state were deadly because their critique led to crisis, the formation of a state ever threatened by fanatic mobs of critics and deemed illegitimate, forever failing to fulfil the utopian task of moralizing society for the betterment of the people. Furthermore, the utopians underplayed the risks involved by an overextended state committed to what was ultimately a moral mission, the fostering of a particular grouping's sense of social morality.

The consequences of such ideologies became visible with a shocking immediacy during the French Revolution. Koselleck, like Edmund Burke, traced the Terror to the naive idiocy of those who called themselves philosophers, gathering in social settings to put the world to rights by what they called reasoned argument, whereas in practice they were laying the foundations of the French revolutionary Terror. An ultimately unwinnable ideological war defined the modern state after the Enlightenment utopians took power during the French Revolution. The Terror itself, justified by subsequent generations of philosophers as a necessary element of a successful movement for social transformation, paved the way for Nazis, Soviet communists, and Chinese Maoists, some of whose horrors had been observed by Koselleck at first hand.

Koselleck developed a view of history and of past politics and its relationship with the present that serves to distinguish *Begriffsgeschichte* from alternative approaches to political thought. The difference can be said to be attitudinal rather than methodological. The distinctiveness came from the definition of modernity. Koselleck called the period in Germany between 1750 and 1850 the *Sattelzeit* (saddle-period), signifying a transition from the early modern to the modern world. Although it was vital to be attuned to the Greek and Latin origins of concepts and the transformation of meanings by use in Old German or English texts, the period of fundamental change occurred between the 18th and 19th centuries. It was then that the modern language of politics was formulated.

Industry (*Industrie, Gewerbe*), from being a term signifying labour or activity in the context of the agrarian household, came to be associated with a particular organization of society as a whole, characterized by institutions employing the mass of productive workers contributing to national economic output and therefore national power. The point about such conceptual change was that it occurred against a background of the speeding up of time itself, both in the sense of the extent of social change through industrial revolution and also through what was termed the 'temporalization of concepts', meaning that the dominant political ideologies of the 19th century such as socialism or liberalism viewed the past from the vantage point that it was inferior to an anticipated future, soon to be realized and altogether redemptive for humanity. The tragedy of present politics from Koselleck's point of view was that political action was justified and indeed determined by a sense of the future, rather than the messy and chaotic realities of the present as constructed through a deep knowledge of the past.

In all of his subsequent work from the 1960s to the end of his life—he moved from Heidelberg to a chair at the new university of Bielefeld in 1973—Koselleck emphasized that the extent to which an ideology underpinning political practice was infused with future-oriented utopian promises of salvation determined the range of actions deemed to be vital in the exercise of politics. This is complicated but can easily be unpacked.

The legal ideology underpinning the actions of lawyers or that enunciated by reforming bureaucrats entailed a sense of time that was far slower than that demanded by the new social movements which divided Germany in the 1970s. Revolutionaries and the ideologies they peddled insisted that time be speeded up so everyone could enjoy the utopia on the horizon. Ideologies fought one another conceptually. Their battles could be charted through the synchronous analysis of language in time. Yet they could not be understood without diachronic analysis too, derived from the study of the conceptual sense of history and of the desired or likely future. Arguments in politics had to be seen to be layered, having multiple meanings depending upon the angle from which they were viewed. The actions of any human being had to be related to both their specific past and their sense of the likely future.

Every human being had a sense of friend and foe; conflict was inevitable and never resolved without accepting the permanency of difference. Koselleck was bitter about those who claimed that societal harmony was both possible and realizable, a sure sign that their practitioners were selling religion rather than knowledge. Human societies were always permeated by inequalities and ranks, existing in different forms and entailing greater or lesser iniquities, and forever generating social action and social conflict. Egalitarianism for Koselleck was among the most dangerous modern ideologies because it was the most dismissive of the past and naive about the future, and thereby doomed to a failure which brought with it the justification of extremism.

Koselleck's perspective meant that there were no boundaries to his work. Some events could never be put into words, language could not capture them, including the experience of terror and genocide. He was interested in the manifestations of ideology in every form, from dreams, memories, and representations of sex to war memorials and images of death, legal institutions, and propaganda. Manifestations of the ideological wars of the 20th century could be found everywhere, with their competing moral crusades and willingness to justify any practice in politics in order to foster their particular sense of morality, falsely described as objectively true, good, and worthy.

This was evident in Koselleck's brilliant essay collections, appearing in English as *Futures Past* (1985), *The Practice of Conceptual History: Timing History, Spacing Concepts* (2002), and *Sediments of Time: On Possible Histories* (2018). History had no inherent meaning, theological significance, law-based teleology, or direction. Yet the study of human experience through history gave an infinitely more realistic sense of the likely evolution of political ideologies and the extent to which they were fanatic. In Koselleck's hands *Begriffsgeschichte* refined the approaches of Dilthey and of Meinecke. For Koselleck the transformation of the use of concepts over time facilitated far greater nuance and complication into writing about the history of political thought, far less order and confident generalization, far more precise evidence, and far more pessimism about modern politics.

Unsurprisingly, there were calls for the application of the techniques of *Begriffsgeschichte* to other countries, as occurred in Rolf Reichardt's *Handbuch politisch-sozialer Grundbegriffe in Frankreich 1680–1820*, the Netherlands book series 'Reeks Nederlandse Begripsgeschiedenis' in the 1990s devoted to the concepts of fatherland, liberty, citizen, and civilization, Melvin Richter's *History of Political and Social Concepts* (1995), and the formation of The History of Political and Social Concepts Group based in Finland with the journal *Contributions to the History of Concepts*.

One of the issues faced by scholars interested in the history of concepts has been long-standing, from the editors of the *Geschichtliche Grundbegriffe* onwards: whether concepts mapped social change or whether they caused it. Did ideas constituted conceptually form a core of meaning available to historical actors who could then alter the meaning through semantic deviation and innovation? If this was the case, as Koselleck argued, then the study of political thought could be divorced from a situational context defined by social analysis. Although events could interrupt and transform ideas, social history did not lead the way because concepts established a range of possible actions through which change in history could be charted. The history of political thought, itself a branch of conceptual history, became an independent discipline of singular significance.

Chapter 7
Michel Foucault and governmentality

Foucault and *Epistémè*

Michel Foucault is often associated with the poststructuralist and postmodernist ideas espoused by a diverse group including Jacques Derrida, Gilles Deleuze, and Jean-François Lyotard, whose famous 1979 *La condition postmoderne* gave common currency to the term postmodern. Derrida's *De la grammatologie* (*Of Grammatology*, 1967) pithily encapsulated the manifesto of the group, 'il n'y a pas de hors-texte [there is nothing outside of the text]', making it possible to proclaim the death of the author. Texts contributed to mental climates in diverse ways, having lives of their own and being open to infinite interpretations, interpretations which themselves were forever being adapted to the passage of time and alteration of circumstance.

Derrida's innovative approach to the study of texts he termed 'arche-writing', revealed through scrutiny of Rousseau's *Essay on the Origin of Languages*. Derrida claimed an author's intentions were constrained by the language and logic which he or she relied upon in the expression of his or her ideas; the full meaning, once textual deconstruction was undertaken, could be revealed only once it was accepted that a text might well step beyond the limits upon it imagined by the author. Author and text needed to be distinguished from one another; no interpretation could ever be said to be exhaustive. Study of the intentions of the author was necessary but insufficient to determine meaning. Nor could meaning be derived from class consciousness defined by reference to an author's biography or to his or her unconscious studied psychoanalytically. Texts were indeterminate. They might even be at war with themselves, containing multiple meanings operating against one another at the same point in time or as understood by readers themselves in distinct situations.

Although there was overlap between the way Foucault sought to recover the meaning of texts and that of Derrida, he needs to be set apart from poststructuralist thought, partly because he ploughed a furrow that itself underwent substantial change, but also because his approach to the study of ideas in general, and politics in particular, was very different, establishing a legacy that is probably the most influential today from a global perspective.

Foucault in his early works saw ideas about politics as being derived from comprehensive bodies of knowledge specific to particular historical epochs. He called these bodies of knowledge epistemological fields or *epistémè*, the Greek term for knowledge. *Epistémè* were discernible through the study of signs and language. They altered over time and were the product of a variety of factors, many of which were random. *Epistémè* at a point in time determined what was deemed to be rational and justifiable as a social practice. *Epistémè* were forever being challenged and ultimately crumbled, to be replaced by another dominant *epistémè* which itself became dominant and then died. In unearthing the *epistémè* behind social actions and political structures Foucault was revealing what was actually happening behind the rhetoric about science and knowledge, neither of which Foucault believed had any objective existence.

One reason for the popularity of Foucault's ideas was that he uncovered the world behind the veil. Revealing the hidden social order and the actuality of things was a commonplace of Marxist thought, which greatly influenced the young Foucault, who had been a close friend to Louis Althusser. In his later works Foucault abandoned the *epistémè*, favouring, instead, the Nietzschean idea of genealogy, seeing genealogies composed of warring discourses.

Foucault was born in 1926 at Poitiers to a middle-class family and educated ultimately at the École Normale Supérieure at Paris, where he fell under the spell of the Hegel scholar Jean-Hippolyte, and Althusser, a leading French communist and dazzlingly original interpreter of Marx. Studying both philosophy and psychology, Foucault was fascinated by conceptions of the normal and abnormal, leading to his first book, *Maladie mentale et personalité* (*Mental Illness and Personality*, 1954), which identified the imprisonment of those deemed to have mental pathologies to be a grotesque evil of capitalism. It was his most Marxist work. Foucault then published *Folie et déraison: histoire de la folie à l'âge classique* (1961; translated as *Madness and Civilization* in 1964) and *Naissance de la clinique: une archéologie du regard médical* (1963) (*Birth of the Clinic: An Archaeology of Medical Perception*, 1972), which showed that medieval and early modern conceptions of madness were redescribed in the 18th century as dangerous illnesses requiring radical cures or the removal of the 'patient' from society, up to the time of Philippe Pinel's setting free of the 'mad' imprisoned at *La Bicêtre* in 1794.

In the modern age of the 19th century up to 1950, the mad were no longer tortured but were rather collected together in asylums from the detritus of capitalist society and those who refused to conform. Foucault lauded those, such as Gérard de Nerval, the Marquis de Sade, or Friedrich Nietzsche, who, in seeing behind the curtain, revealed the truth about society and attacked the modern rationality that justified those practices of isolation and incarceration.

Foucault began to term his approach to the past 'archaeological' in his grander works published while he was working on reason and madness, *Naissance de la clinique: une archéologie du regard médical* (1963), *Les mots et les choses: une archéologie des sciences humaines* (1966), and *L'archéologie du savoir* (1969). *Les mots et les choses* (*The Order of Things*) scrutinized the history of the human sciences devoted to man as a being who lived, produced, and spoke, enjoyed life, labour, and language, and thereby could be seen from the perspective of biology, economics, and culture. Foucault argued that in seeking truth, a constructed concept that in fact did not exist, the purveyors of the human sciences were deluding themselves. What they were doing was determined by the dominant *epistémè* of the period in question.

A parallel might be drawn between Foucault's notion of *epistémè* and Thomas Kuhn's idea of a paradigm, the hidden assumptions behind scientific practices that shaped perceptions of what was rational and valid, defining a normal science before being refuted and replaced by an alternative paradigm. Foucault's *epistémè* were, however, less sharply delineated, less rigorously organized, less coherent. Their collapse did not come through refutation but was rather arbitrary, characterized by rupture and rogue discontinuities. No baton of discernible knowledge was being passed on from human society to society. No progress was being made. There was no pattern to history at all. Foucault's radical conclusion, which drew an enormous amount of attention, was that there were no human sciences in the sense of definable subjects over time. Notions of objective knowledge, objectivity in any form, were fundamentally meaningless. There were no real facts. There was no 'real' reality. Defences of an autonomous and creative subject called 'Man' had to be abandoned because the very idea of a 'subject' did not exist.

Foucault and archaeology

Foucault was denounced in many circles, including by Marxists, variously as a sceptic, thoroughgoing relativist, or Nietzschean nihilist. He was also attacked for not having any solutions to the problems of society, being a nay-sayer and a critic rather than someone who saw the role of the intellectual to offer solutions to the problems of the present. Indeed, if there was no meaning to philosophy or history, Foucault could actually be said to be defending the existing social order because it was just as valid as any other social order.

That Foucault rejected such criticism became clear with the appearance of *L'archéologie du savoir* (*The Archaeology of Knowledge*) in 1969. History, rather than be seen as a process of evolving languages and signs creating meaning, needed instead, Foucault argued, to be seen as a genealogy of struggle, of a will to power in Nietzsche's sense of an irrational motivating force, and with it domination and control. The outcome of any struggle was determined by the capacity of dominant forces in particular societies to repress, control, conceal, and expurgate those marginal to them. In addition to the bare power relations in existence in a society, power relations that shaped not only institutional arrangements but social and individual outlooks, customs, habits, manners, and attitudes, the way people engaged with themselves and the world, it was also necessary to take into account the strategies devised by the powerful to justify their practices and the tactics employed to carry out their actions. Strategies and tactics were naturally deployed by the oppressed too to defend themselves or alter their circumstances.

Oppression and control were not for Foucault straightforwardly identifiable in any society. Looking at a society did not reveal, as it did for Marxists, those utterly oppressed and the oppressors, two great classes fighting to change or maintain the world. Rather, for Foucault, power relations were everywhere, in every walk of life, in every human interaction. Sometimes control was easy to spot, sometimes near impossible because it was the very fabric of social existence.

The subjects of archaeology were discourses, statements, events, and 'archives', the system of structures that generated social meaning, making sense of human statements and giving prestige to particular perspectives upon the world. Rather than being defined by language, discursive practices which humans employed in their will to power shaped and were shaped by technical, practical, economic, political, and social factors.

Foucault continued to reject approaches to the history of political thought founded upon an author's intentions, the extent of his or her innovation, and the search for the origins of ideas in the past. The author for Foucault remained dead. There were no basic historically identifiable narratives which could be relied upon to make sense of the past but rather perpetual identifiable continuities and discontinuities, hidden and revealed power relations, an enormous web of practice and discourse, all of which merited analysis and investigation. Enunciated statements were the foundation of Foucault's approach. These had to be interrogated to identify discursive practices, the 'anonymous historical rules, always specific in time and place, and which, for a given period and within a social, economic, and geographic or linguistic area, define the framework within which the enunciative functions are exercised'. The linking thread between Foucault's later writings and earlier work was his praise for divergence, the feeling of not fitting, or a sense of being oppressed. Such senses, he argued, were far more prevalent than anyone had recognized hitherto.

Normalization and biopolitics

From the beginning of the 1970s, when Foucault arrived as the leading professor in the History of Systems of Thought at the Collège de France, and for the remainder of the decade, the relationship between discourse and power was at the very centre of the analysis of contemporary and historical issues. These were addressed in hugely popular lectures by Foucault—the holder of the chair was required to teach for twenty-six hours per year, half of which were to be given as public lectures describing ongoing research. The lectures ranged widely across different subjects and fields, within lectures and year-by-year, covering subjects as diverse as political economy, governance, psychological power, social and psychological 'deviance', and the human subject. Discourse for Foucault was 'controlled, selected, organized and redistributed according to a certain number of procedures' setting out rules ranging from logic and grammar to censorship that determined the validity of the discourse and its function in society. The 'policing' of language and social practices had to be sought out and named.

Foucault called his method genealogical, which he described in his significant article 'Nietzsche, Genealogy, History' of 1971. He continued to be fascinated by unreason, the critics of contemporary rationalities, and those who lived in the manner of the Greek/Roman god Dionysus/Bacchus devoted to wine, fertility, madness, ecstasy, and sybaritic existence. Lives lived in such a fashion, Foucault argued, were more powerful than had been recognized. Rebelling by living such lives had the potential to change the world for the better, freeing humanity from the shackles of discourse that enforced conformity in accordance with the demands of existing systems of power.

One of the most influential of all of Foucault's books resulted, *Surveiller et punir: naissance de la prison* (1975), translated as *Discipline and Punish*, which, in repeating the central argument from his earlier *Folie et déraison dans l'âge classique*, distinguished between the classical era up to the end of the 18th century and the modern era. Whereas in *Madness and Civilization* Foucault was interested in the development of therapies to treat the 'mentally ill', therapies that hid away the mad and aimed to reshape their personalities, rendering them docile and obedient, so that they could be returned to 'normal' life, in *Discipline and Punish* he turned his attention to prisons and legal punishments.

Discipline and Punish showed how the classical era was characterized by brutal forms of punishment—torture, beheadings, drawing and quartering—against the transgressors of authority. The modern era, which saw the introduction of the modern prison and the decline in the uses of corporal punishments, was perceived to have been characterized by the rise of compassion and reform, enunciated in congratulatory register by 19th- and 20th-century commentators. Foucault argued that the techniques of control were in fact far greater, demanding docile bodies to be observed, documented, and shaped in accordance with the needs of the dominant knowledge system. He condemned 'the carceral city' dedicated to 'the fabrication of the disciplinary individual' in which 'central and centralized humanity' experienced 'bodies and forces subjected by multiple mechanisms of "incarceration", objects for discourses that are in themselves elements for this strategy'.

Discipline and Punish was followed by studies of what Foucault termed 'the power of normalization and the formation of knowledge in modern society' in lectures of 1976 and 1977–8 respectively, *Il faut défendre la société* (*Society Must Be Defended*, translated in 2003) and *Sécurité, territoire, population* (1977–8) (*Security, Territory, Population*, translated in 2007). Foucault had by this time become a cult figure. His lectures were widely lauded, popularized, and attended by more people than could ever be fitted into theatres. The lectures were concerned more and more with the regulations and practices employed by modern states to discipline their populations and make adherence to authority habitual. Modern states were also, Foucault claimed, devoted to making their populations pursue particular forms of living, prescribing every aspect of the lived existence. The prescribed social practices were held to be so rational and necessary for life that they became internalized by many individual selves who inhabited the state.

To the manifold direct disciplinary techniques Foucault had outlined in *Discipline and Punish* he added 'biopower' in his lectures of the late 1970s. Biopower was a set of mechanisms, as he put it in a lecture of 11 January 1978, 'through which the basic biological features of the human species became the object of a political strategy, of a general strategy of power, or, in other words, how, starting from the eighteenth century, modern Western societies took on board the fundamental biological fact that human beings are a species'.

Foucault discussed the establishment of towns in early modern Europe as organizations for the regulation of social, moral, economic, and administrative space. The mechanisms of biopower were employed in towns in accordance with imperatives incumbent upon their inhabitants to become involved in commerce and to maintain social hygiene. Biopower was therefore the regularization of all of the members of a society by what Foucault called 'governmentality', the techniques and procedures designed to govern humans in particular societies as children, worshippers, moral adults, members of households, as individuals and as subjects or citizens of nation states.

Evidence of growing emphasis upon governmentality and an indication of what it entailed was provided by the new 18th-century science of political economy. The science of political economy was a form of knowledge that facilitated increased governmentality by scrutinizing populations and measuring the behaviour of the people. Equally, it emphasized the need for a secure state able to defend itself using its economic power. Governmentality tended to develop hand-in-hand with governmental apparatuses and systems of knowledge devoted to investigation, evaluation, and control.

Governmentality, if successful, meant that humans defined themselves in accordance with the dictates of the directing rulers of the state, down to their very sense of self. So pervasive were the forces of governmentality that Foucault argued that even the purported growth of individualism and individuality under 18th-century and 19th-century capitalism was itself in reality part of a broader process of homogenization and regularization. People might think they were rebelling or pursuing practices that went against the cultural grain. Yet they were in fact unwittingly maintaining the existing system of coercive control. Rebellion was acceptable in areas of life that did not substantially matter to governments, especially in terms of threatening the state and the power structures that formed it.

Foucault's solution to the problem of oppression via governmentality lay in the promotion of 'new forms of subjectivity through refusal of this kind of individuality which has been imposed on us for several centuries'. Turning to the history of sex and sexuality in his three-volume *The History of Sexuality* to illustrate what he meant, Foucault's final works contrasted eastern practices dedicated to sexual experimentation and enjoyment with ever-growing western control over bodies and minds. He had come to the conclusion that even perceived practices of western sexual liberation in contemporary times served to enforce the existing structures of power. Foucault looked to the Graeco-Roman world, in which sex was a means of creating character, and contrasted their sexual practices with modern impulses, which Foucault traced to St Augustine, to use sex to normalize behaviour in societies.

Foucault and the history of political thought

What was Foucault's contribution to the history of political thought beyond the methods he developed for the study and scrutiny of the realities of life both historic and in the present?

Many answers could be given but one way of thinking about the question is to look at Foucault's treatment of Machiavelli. For Foucault, Straussian claims about Machiavelli's modern perspective upon the world made no sense. Machiavelli's prince had seen himself to be secure in being sovereign over a particular territory. This for Foucault was the end of a significant story in the history of politics. As he put it, 'far from thinking that Machiavelli opens up the field of political thought to modernity, I would say that he marks instead the end of an age, or anyway that he reaches the highest point of a moment in which the problem was actually that of the safety of the Prince and his territory'.

According to Foucault, in the century after Machiavelli commerce changed everything: 'we see the emergence of a completely different problem that is no longer that of fixing and demarcating the territory, but of allowing circulations to take place, of controlling them, sifting the good and the bad, ensuring that things are always in movement'. Territorial integrity no longer mattered. What did was the security of the population and of those who governed it. In other words, Machiavelli's world succumbed to the growth of biopolitics. Governmentality became the central function of the state. As Foucault noted in a lecture of 25 January 1978, it was the new focus upon the governance of domestic populations that caused 'the transition from natural history to biology, from the analysis of wealth to political economy, and from general grammar to historical philology'. Traditional systems of knowledge were transformed towards sciences of life, labour and production, and language, the better to foster governmentality and its ethos.

In Foucault's view there was a contradiction in modern liberalism that needed to be revealed. The institutions of the liberal world in the West, from rights to the welfare state and rules to moderate the boom and bust of economic cycles, were justified 'to avoid the reduction of freedom that would be entailed by the transition to socialism, fascism, or National Socialism'. Foucault claimed that liberal institutions and practices, 'the mechanisms for producing freedom, precisely those that are called upon to manufacture this freedom, actually produce destructive effects which prevail over the very freedom they are supposed to produce'. He predicted future 'crises of liberalism' not because of capitalism but because of the more encompassing oppressive effects of governmentality of which capitalism was a part.

Foucault was also concerned about a new species of liberalism, which is now widely termed neoliberalism, in which the state existed 'under the supervision of the market rather than a market supervised by the state'. Such developments were far more dangerous, Foucault observed, in the United States of America than in Europe. European liberalism, he argued, had always sought, whatever it did in practice, to limit state power. European liberals called upon governments to refrain from intervening in the domains of society that were better left to markets. In the United States, for Foucault, liberalism had justified independence in the 18th-century revolution and then formed the American state. Neoliberalism as it was coming to be known in North America was different from classical liberalism because it called upon the market to measure and evaluate the activity of the state, as if sitting in perpetual judgement.

Foucault was first and foremost a critic of existing and historic societies, providing the tools to reveal the truth behind the curtain and to identify the actual existing forms of injustice and oppression that were all too often ignored or presumed not to exist. His work has inspired two generations of scholars and commentators. It is now pervasive at least in the sense of being an acknowledged influence upon the work of legions of people interested in the history of political thought. Moving from a general sense of influence to specific scholarship is more difficult to chart, partly because Foucault's mind saw random ideas jump all over the place and his diffuse writing reflected this, generating connections that few have the imagination to see.

This means that there is no such thing as a Foucauldian method or interpretation. Rather, there are perspectives or approaches that emerge having engaged with Foucault. An example can be found in Keith Tribe's Foucault-inspired critique of neoliberalism. According to Tribe, the neoliberal charting of a world of economic rationality eradicated the public space formerly occupied by politics, virtue, and ethics. In so doing, a language of politics identifiable since the ancient Greeks was being written over and the monuments of republican argument in the United States, the Declaration of Independence, the Constitution and the Bill of Rights, were being set to one side. Neoliberalism, from the point of view of Foucault's definition of governmentality, could be redescribed as 'un-American in the most negative sense possible'.

Chapter 8
Globality, morality, and the future

The relevance of the history of political thought

Since the late 1960s research in the history of political thought has increasingly been inspired by the writings of Strauss, Foucault, Koselleck, and Cambridge School authors. Although highly distinctive as approaches to the study of the past and political thought, each of the pioneers took history seriously and sought to reconstruct the meaning of texts through analysis of their original ideological contexts and to develop a perspective on the present informed by what had gone before. Notably, each figure was critical of what has come to be termed 'globalization'. Despite the rejection of Marxist categories for interrogating history, and proletarian revolution as a mechanism of purposive social transformation, the world created by capitalism has continued to be attacked for its endemic war and fanatical politics, its disdain for the past, and seeming inability to learn from history.

Either by revealing the overwhelming power of the irrational in the present or by recovering lost traditions that could be favourably compared with those contemporary politicians blindly adhered to, the history of political thought trained scholars to see the problems of contemporary society differently through an understanding of how related issues had been addressed in history. The point was never to be merely critical, although it is always useful to see through crude ideological world views. Rather, the history of political thought allows the range of possible political actions in given circumstances to be charted and the likelihood of their success evaluated. The history of political thought equally has predictive power, providing a sense of strengths and weaknesses in particular societies; above all, it provides information about the nature and likelihood of political crises.

If you know about the history of political ideas you can begin to perceive politics contextually: topics presented as new can be seen and better understood as contributing to a longer-standing debate or set of debates. Take the common western presentation of politics in China as being akin to what used to be termed an oriental despotism, meaning a state lacking elections, being ruled autocratically, being corrupt, and ultimately lacking legitimacy. The reality, it has been argued, especially by certain commentators who have experience of East and West, is very different. The rule of the Communist Party in China can in fact be justified if seen as a meritocracy in which only those who do a good job in governing at lower levels of society are allowed to ascend to higher office. Failure at any level is punished with the loss of office. Sometimes government officers have been imprisoned if their exercise of power led to disaster, as in the instance of the 2011 high-speed train collision in the industrial port city of Wenzhou in Zhejiang province.

One consequence of this meritocracy, it is asserted, is that those from extremely poor backgrounds can rise to the top, if they governed well at lower levels and were given greater responsibility in consequence. The critical point might be made that such a justification seems to apply primarily to men alone but this can be said of most government systems; the issue here is that, notwithstanding this gender skew, meritocracy and upwards mobility translate into popular legitimacy, in part because the populace recognizes that those who failed to follow the public good would not remain long in office.

Such a picture might be contrasted with the democratic politics of the West where a man—and it has tended predominantly to be men in every political system—might find himself president having had no experience of public office or any education in governance in accordance with the public good. How could a system be justified in which, to give the example from Ukraine, the current political class is so despised for being self-serving that the populace elects a person whose qualifications are that he played a successful president in a television series? Moving to the United States, even those who had been in politics for some time, such as George W. Bush or Barack Obama, had limited experience of practical governance when they entered the highest office, by contrast with their Chinese counterparts, who were experts in a manner that was rare elsewhere (Joe Biden is the exception).

In Britain a slightly different situation pertains. Almost everyone that Britain's Prime Minister Margaret Thatcher knew or worked alongside had been to the same small number of private schools and then to the universities of Oxford or Cambridge. Thatcher's world, to any observer, gave every impression of being an elite enjoying top positions in every branch of society. Should Britain then be described as a democracy or an aristocracy or even a plutocracy, especially given that the same point could be made about the subsequent governments of Tony Blair, David Cameron, Theresa May, or Boris Johnson? Is it significant that 300 years ago Robert Walpole became the first prime minister and was educated as a King's Scholar at Eton and that exactly the same education was received by Boris Johnson, the difference being that Walpole attended Cambridge while Johnson went to Oxford?

Chinese commentators often make the point that politicians or business leaders in the West are never punished for failure.

However terrible their decisions or however unpopular they might find themselves to be, they could always find lucrative posts in industry on leaving office and enjoy salaries that ordinary individuals could only dream about. In business a common outcome sees them moved from one executive board to another. In England knighthoods, medals, and other 'gongs' for 'service' would only in the most exceptional cases be taken away. China, by contrast, even though a revolving door between office and corporations has always existed, is said to be far more egalitarian with regard to recruitment and had a far stronger sense of public service.

Contemporary evidence about the treatment of minority communities in China challenges the evidence of apologists. Widespread corruption is acknowledged, as it always is across the commercialized globe. Environmental damage through rapid industrialization too remains a real problem in China. The main claim remains, however, that an independent observer might well come to the view that the Chinese form of government remains superior to that of western democracies according to the measures of public service and in being, for men at least, a meritocracy.

The conclusion might then be arrived at that China has developed a tradition of politics entirely alien to that of the West. This would be a mistake. In fact, the notion of officials only being able to stand for office if they had proved themselves at lower governmental levels is commonplace in the history of western political thought. In his original plan for a new form of government in late 18th-century France, Sieyès outlined such an idea. He was drawing on Jean-Jacques Rousseau's work on a reformed form of government in Poland. The German philosopher Hegel soon followed them. Positive descriptions of Chinese meritocracy could be said to be Hegelian in the identification of an educated political/bureaucratic class enunciating and putting into practice the common good.

Supporters of the Chinese model often replicate one of the standard critiques of representative democracy in the 18th century, that it was the easiest of political systems to transform into a narrow aristocracy, since the people tended always to vote for the rich, the famous, or the prominent in society. This meant that in a representative democracy it was always difficult to ensure that politicians favoured the public good rather than their private interests dressed up as the good of all. The counter-argument to Hegel's rational bureaucracy was naturally that it too might well succumb to sinister interests, as Marx later claimed was the case in Prussia. During the same period Bentham argued that the only way of being certain that the public good was being followed in practice was to define it forensically; this was the goal of utilitarian philosophy.

A significant fact about the field of the history of political thought today is that the disciplinary approaches developed since the 1960s are under assault. One assertion has it that historians of political thought are not critical enough. Progress is said to have occurred in society and what went before reveals abuses and injustice. Written histories ought then to focus upon recent improvements and the superiority of the present, especially regarding human rights. Such an approach can be used to demand further improvement towards an egalitarian utopia. Liberal, neoliberal, and Marxist approaches to the history of political thought owe much to this view of the past, commonplace in studies of politics across certain ahistorical social sciences and among political philosophers. One danger in current trends to moralize history, sometimes by taking what is termed a 'global' standpoint, is that the same kinds of utopian and teleological history are replicated just as the exponents of the new histories believe they are doing something different.

Another attack is a variant of the old Marxist demand that historical techniques be used, as E. P. Thompson put it, to rescue individuals from 'the enormous condescension of posterity'. Thompson's *The Making of the English Working Class* (1963), where this point was made, brilliantly recovered many of the lost voices of ordinary people engaged in what he perceived was 'class struggle before class' in late 18th- and early 19th-century British rebel movements, gradually becoming aware of the historic role of the working class in accordance with the Marxist schema. Thompson was less successful in identifying what he called 'moral economy' in the history of political and economic thought, a putative category that he argued characterized the world before justifications of laissez-faire, absolute property rights, and selfishness began to dominate political thought. Thompson's category of moral economy was largely empty but his work inspired a generation of scholars to follow in his footsteps and become social historians. Exponents of subaltern studies, such as Ranajit Guha, have been following Thompson's injunction in demanding the recovery of the voices of the oppressed across the globe and especially the victims of colonial misrule. Such work is to be welcomed in the same manner as Thompson's once was. The presumption is sometimes made that this approach is distinctive methodologically. This is not the case; subaltern studies follow the approaches that have flourished since the 1960s in broadening the canon and recovering lost traditions and neglected perspectives.

Global histories of political thought

This book is not organized around a canon of dead white male philosophers. Has it nevertheless reinforced the stereotype because the leading practitioners of the history of political thought are almost as likely as their subject matter to be male and European, if not in all cases deceased? In place of Plato, Aristotle, Machiavelli, Hobbes, Rousseau, and such like we get Strauss, Pocock, Skinner, Koselleck, and Foucault. It is frequently asserted that any group of white males translates into a lack of diversity of viewpoint. Perspectives are of course influenced by being male, white, and living in particular historical circumstances. In the case of these authors, the diversity of ideological contexts in which they have formulated their ideas is marked. This is not to say that the new contexts of the present will fail to add to the study of the history of political thought and its understanding. We are, for example, only now more fully appreciating the role of women in the history of political thought and the significance of gender. The diversity of practitioners and contextualist methodological practices is to be welcomed.

The related criticism levelled against the history of political thought, as noted, is that it is primarily Eurocentric and secondarily overly focused upon North America. It is normally accepted, however, that European and North American political thought remains worthy of further scrutiny. After all, we still do not know enough about the transformation of European political thought, as Pocock has put it, 'from a Mediterranean context, polytheist, philosophical and rhetorical, to a European [context], monotheist, theological and juristic'. The criticism remains that too many male philosophers of European origin are still particularly venerated within a list of political theorists deemed most relevant. Happily, numerous scholars are working on non-European political thought who have been trained in the methods of study developed since the 1960s. We know far more than ever before about, for example, Confucian, Buddhist, Shinto, Islamic, and Orthodox political thought.

Political thought has come to exist in different places with distinct contexts. These contexts can be isolated or dynamically interact with political thought in other places with their own distinctive histories. Political thought might have distinct meanings in different forms of society. In a society entirely divorced from European norms comprehension cannot be reduced to western categories. There is little to disagree, therefore, with Andrew Sartori's recent assertions about global intellectual history as they might be applied to the history of political thought, that there are diverse worlds each with a distinctive philosophical formation, that connections between these worlds merit scrutiny, and that valid comparative techniques need to be developed. In other words, it is worthwhile to study the globalization of trade, political machinations, NGOs, and the ideologies associated with them, of which 'capitalism' is one sort; such aspirations align entirely with the methods developed by historians of political thought.

Sartori has made the further point that 'global' ideas cannot be reduced to their 'western' provenance. Somehow a 'global' perspective needs to be developed that allows us to identify our own prejudices. The last point is significant because of the additional critique of Eurocentrism that it is necessarily racist, blinkered, imperialist, and colonialist. In short, Sartori repeats accusations about implicit or explicit Orientalism made famous by Edward Said's book of 1978 subtitled 'Western Conceptions of the Orient'. It should be noted that Said was himself questioned for turning history into a morality tale in which the anti-orientalists became objective, ahistorical, and pristine moral subjects expounding a 'view from nowhere'. Sartori's defence of the global is important because such categories offer the hope of grounding anti-orientalism historically.

The problem remains that 'the global' in this second sense, as a methodology and moral crusade now besetting political thought and its history, is singularly difficult to associate with an identifiable methodology or obvious insight into politics. For Sartori the global cannot be 'an implausible state of exhaustively networked planetary integration'. Rather, he defines the global as 'the peculiar mode of social abstraction characteristic of capitalist society that defies reduction to spatial or scalar delimitation'. Such definitions, bidding 'chapeau' to Marx, remind us that the study of the global is not at all new. The word globalization is new and signifies an unparalleled intensity of interconnectedness of individuals and nations, normally dated as a process commencing in the 17th century. Commentary on the process of globalization was certainly going on in the 18th century. By the 19th century the implications of the global world were the foundation of new accounts of ideological change, for example Hegel's *Philosophy of Right (Rechtphilosophie)* of 1820 and his *Lectures on the Philosophy of World History (Vorlesungen über die Philosophie der Weltgeschichte)* given at Berlin University in the 1820s. Hegel's speculations led to the most ambitious ever demand for global transformation, Marx's and Engel's *Communist Manifesto* of 1848.

There is kinship between speculation about global political thought defined in this moral manner and the Marxist inheritance. One of the obvious dangers, Pocock has warned, is that the quest for the global 'entails a critique if not an abandonment of the concept of "context"'. Just as Marxism in particular countries justified the bludgeoning of traditional religion, politics, philosophy, and society in the name of the coming global transition to socialism, so there is a possibility that global political thought is similarly dismissive of the local, traditional, and long established. If this turned out to be the case then global impulses in political thought would be the intellectual equivalent of global capitalism, rooting out diversity, homogenizing cultures, and demanding a unity of thought and practice. Once again Pocock has voiced this fear, entailing for him the loss of history and therefore the loss of meaningful political identity:

> In the history now ascendant, the 'imperial' and 'post-colonial' periods are succeeded, with such rapidity that 'we' ourselves are disempowered by it, by a global capitalism that not only unifies the planet's economy but offers to supply it with an instant culture, manufactured by the global market and perpetually reproduced as commodity to meet the market's need for constant self-transformation. In such a world politics and history can have no place, if they are thought of as products of spatial-temporal cultures possessing their own means of duration and decision.

The study of the pre-global world and its political cultures risks being shouted down by those who do not understand that a historical sense appreciative of diverse contexts can lead to moderation through knowledge of the contextually contingent nature of all of our beliefs. If globality becomes an intolerant ideology describing itself as all-seeing and objective then everyone will suffer. We will have turned our backs upon the critique of globalizations, which has been one of the most important consequences of the history of political thought since the later 20th century.

Moral judgements in the history of political thought

Should we avoid the study of dead white males whose questionable and sometimes abhorrent morals, at odds with the values we defend in the present, ought simply to be forgotten? Take the example of Benjamin Constant. Constant was for much of his life a rake and a libertine. He was addicted to gambling and for a long period of time his debts were paid by the chief among his many lovers, Anne-Louise Germaine de Staël (one of the wealthiest women in Europe). At some point de Staël accepted that Constant's behaviour was too much to take. When she was near death in 1817 she refused to see him. Constant is, of course, lauded as one of the founders of modern liberalism and as a champion of rights, liberty, and representative government. Should we read him, given his manifest sexism and amorality? Should his works be expunged from reading lists in the history of political thought? This is a question now shaping the field, but it is not a new one. All societies formulate stories about where they come from. Authors come into fashion and go out of fashion, often for ad hoc reasons.

Across Christian Europe in previous centuries what type of faith someone adhered to determined whether and where they would be studied. Catholic universities would either avoid the Lutheran

Pufendorf or expurgate what they found offensive in his works. Protestant universities would teach Paolo Sarpi's *History of the Council of Trent* (1619) because, despite being a priest, he was seen to have ridiculed the Counter-Reformation. A vast market in hidden best-sellers existed, ranging from pornography to scandal sheets to the works of Machiavelli or Hobbes.

There has always been censorship and official judgement of what kinds of political texts are suitable for the public. Although it is a work of fiction, a good introduction to the kinds of questions dealt with in the history of political thought remains Umberto Eco's *The Name of the Rose* (1980). The novel tells the story of the putting to the torch of a medieval library because of the unorthodox doctrines its ancient manuscripts contained. Eco makes a lot of a lost text of Aristotle's in defence of laughter, which violated a Benedictine monk Jorge of Burgos's obsession with austerity, penitence, and prayer in preparation for the true life to come after the sin and misery of life on earth. Is the lesson then that all societies are subject to what are these days termed purity spirals and that we should not worry about studying the Constants or others like him? I would argue that what Constant wrote about republican fanaticism, about the relationship between religion and politics, and the need for moderation in politics to avoid war at all costs remains worth hearing.

It is always a bad idea to judge the past by the present as that would mean that we cease to be able to use history or to get any benefit from it. The aim should rather be to allow the past to inform the present. Take the case of empire. Empire has become an evil word. There are calls everywhere for the decolonization of thought and practice. This can mean, especially in universities, looking at curricula and deciding to teach texts that relate how dreadful have been the atrocities committed under the guise of empire, how great the exploitation, how violent the oppressors in charge, how awful the lived life within such a form of government. All of this is crucial work; we need to be aware of the terrible things that happened in many imperial systems. It is not, however, everything that there is to say about empire.

For most of human history vast numbers of people have lived under what would now be termed an imperial yoke, lacking any sense of sovereignty. Think of the empires that covered so much of the known ancient world such as the Assyrian, Persian, Macedonian, and Roman. The Umayyad caliphate ranged from the Indus to Iberia. The empire of the Incas stretched across 32 degrees of latitude in 1491, from present-day Ecuador to Chile. In modern times the British Empire, although relatively short-lived, covered a quarter of the terrestrial surface; few of these empires were beset by persistent rebellion. This was not necessarily because humans enjoyed societies where they were perpetually oppressed, powerless, and miserable. Rather, people lived within empires and neither resisted nor emigrated when given the chance because empire was the form of government they associated with peace. If you found yourself living under empire you might find yourself without rights and without liberty. Peace, even when insecure, might well still have been valued. Visions of perpetual peace in the history of political thought have often come down to the justification of the once-significant category in politics, that of universal monarchy. Universal monarchy meant having one ruler of all lands capable of standing above other political figures and having the strength and authority to bring peace.

The linkage between empire and political success is far deeper than might be imagined. Figures akin to universal monarchs are venerated for having brought peace in the origin stories of a multitude of contemporary religions. Prophets and gods bring order where there is chaos. Religion and imperialism have often gone together, fusing proselytizing and war together. Equally, many successful economic organizations, including most contemporary corporations, are said to have been established by individual figures with near mythical capacities for profit and innovation. A charismatic person with the ability to inspire creates a company that is then successful only if it defeats its rivals. The model of universal monarchy predominates across the economy. Almost all corporations are said to be successful if they behave like empires. The chief executive is expected to have singular power, to stand above all others, to make judgements swiftly and efficiently, to adapt to altered circumstances, and above all else to grow the company. It is notable that we venerate the imperial model in the areas of life that supply us with the products we need to live and in the theologies that we have faith in yet do the opposite in politics.

One reason is that monarchs in the establishment of their empires, said to be for the establishment of peace, tend to begin the journey with ceaseless war. Much modern political thought has been concerned with preventing the rise of Caesar figures who promise that they will bring peace and prosperity once the initial wars are won. At the same time as we denigrate empire many of us live under nationalist rulers and populist politicians who promise to make the states in which we live great. Great tends to mean bigger, sooner or later.

None of these arguments, however, should lead us to the conclusion that empires are good. Modern empires especially, in the sense of super-large states, tend to be characterized by homogeneous and superficial cultures. At the same time the process of decolonization, even after the imperial tyranny is thrown off, is normally itself accompanied by war. How many newly liberated states have collapsed into civil war? How many peoples declare themselves free and then decide to take up arms against one another? To students of the history of political thought it is obvious that you cannot simply abolish empire: you have to implement strategies to prevent war from breaking out once the empires are gone.

A second problem with empires has always been that as they are challenged and break apart the field is left open for another imperial power to step into the breach. In the 18th century there was an obsession with the destruction of empires. Thinkers recognized that if the French, for example, emancipated their colonies, as was proposed in the early years of the French Revolution, it would mean in practice that the British would quickly move in. Getting rid of empire risked swapping one oppressive system of rule for another. It is never easy to reject imperial rule and find something better. Declaring empire to be bad and not going further than this amounts to allowing it to continue to thrive.

Historical analysis can entail the enunciation of moral injunctions perceived to be lacking in a society and that ought to be adhered to habitually. When history takes this form there is a danger that species of what might be termed the 'non-history of political thought', because they entail little reflection, suddenly become widespread; they return us to the kinds of teleological, nationalist variants of political argument that have flourished too often in societies that turn their back upon history. The point is worth repeating that we cannot judge the past by the present. Take the case of human consumption of animals. Assume that within two generations it is decided across human societies that eating meat is an evil either because of its environmental consequences, its association with the creation of threatening disease, or because of abhorrence of the violence suffered by animals and the commodification of their lives. Those committed to this point of view may look back negatively upon past thinkers who have lived in cultures dedicated to meat consumption. If the works of thinkers are leafed through and positive comments are found about the consumption of meat does it mean that such authors and their works ought to be cast out and no longer read? No one would gain from such an outcome.

Humans may be at a turning point not only with regard to their capacity to exploit nature or to fill the world with ever more humans, but also in their view of history. The past is simplified and marketed online in small factoid chunks. Morsel history is the result. One of the fundamental problems with present-day politics is that we see it ahistorically. A more general presumption of progress leads us to identify critics of our politics as enemies of our values. The history of political thought counsels against such presuppositions on the grounds that politics, itself fraught with uncertainty and difficulties, cannot be understood in terms of generalizations or universal principles. To make absolute generalizations about current politics is, as the study of the history of political thought makes all too clear, inadvisable.

What then can the history of political thought do for us? It can relate scepticism and uncertainty about our future to parallel fears expressed in the past. It is not the first time in history that we anticipate the likely end of days through political revolution by democratic mobs or autocrats in the guise of military Caesars or super-rich merchant Caesars. Equally commonplace is fanaticism in politics, ever likely to reignite wars of religion. In commercial societies a threat to stability and peace has always existed in the form of the pursuit of baubles and trinkets, which lead people to turn away from their communities and from politics. As dangerous are evangelical schemes of social or global transformation that can readily be sold to the masses by captains of industry or politicians in demagogic mode. In drawing upon the knowledge of the past generated by scrutinizing ideas about politics in their own time, duties and responsibilities (and those of our governments) to one another and to the wider world can be more clearly and realistically perceived.

References

Chapter 2: Definitions and justifications

Barbara Stollberg-Rilinger, 'Weibliche Herrschaft als Ausnahme?
  Maria Theresia und die Geschlechterordnung des 18.
  Jahrhunderts', in Bettina Brau, Jan Kusber, and Matthias
  Schnettger, eds, *Weibliche Herrschaft im 18. Jahrhundert: Maria
  Theresia und Katharina die Große* (Bielefeld: De Gruyter,
  2020), 25 n.
John Dunn, 'Why we Need a Global History of Political Thought', in
  Bela Kaposy, Isaac Nakimovsky, Sophus Reinert, and Richard
  Whatmore, eds, *Markets, Morals and Political Thought: Essays in
  Honour of Istvan Hont* (Cambridge, Mass.: Harvard University
  Press, 2018), 285–307.

Chapter 3: The history of political thought and Marxism

R. G. Collingwood to Chadborne Gilpatric, 17 February 1940, in James
  Connelly, Peter Johnson, and Stephen Leach, eds,
  R. G. Collingwood: A Research Companion (London: Bloomsbury,
  2014), 54.
Istvan Hont, *Politics in Commercial Society: Jean-Jacques Rousseau
  and Adam Smith*, ed. Béla Kapossy and Michael Sonenscher
  (Cambridge, Mass.: Harvard University Press, 2015), 104–6.

Chapter 4: Political philosophers and the history of political thought

Laurence Lampert, 'Strauss's Recovery of Esotericism', in Steven B. Smith, ed., *The Cambridge Companion to Leo Strauss* (Cambridge: Cambridge University Press, 2009), 67.

Harvey C. Mansfield, Conversations with Bill Kristol, May 2015, <https://conversationswithbillkristol.org/wp-content/uploads/2015/05/Mansfield_Strauss_conversations_transcript.pdf>.

Chapter 5: The 'Cambridge School'

Peter Laslett, 'Cambridge and the Social Sciences', *Cambridge Opinion*, 10 Oct 1958, 5–8.

J. G. A. Pocock, 'The Historian as Political Actor in Polity, Society and Academy', in *Political Thought and History: Essays on Theory and Method* (Cambridge: Cambridge University Press, 2009), 217–38.

Chapter 7: Michel Foucault and governmentality

Keith Tribe, 'The Political Economy of Modernity: Foucault's Collège de France Lectures of 1978 and 1979', *Economy and Society*, 38/4 (2009), 679–98.

Chapter 8: Globality, morality, and the future

Andrew Sartori, 'Intellectual History as Global History', in Richard Whatmore and Brian Young, eds, *A Companion to Intellectual History* (London: Wiley, 2015), 201–12.

J. G. A. Pocock, 'On the Unglobality of Contexts: Cambridge Methods and the History of Political Thought', *Global Intellectual History*, 4/1 (2019), 1–14.

Further reading

One way of becoming hooked on the history of political thought is to read some of the classic books mentioned herein, by Hannah Arendt, Isaiah Berlin, John W. Burrow, John Dunn, Michel Foucault, Istvan Hont, Reinhard Koselleck, John Pocock, Judith Shklar, Quentin Skinner, and Leo Strauss. Other works that provide entry points to the subject include David Armitage, *Foundations of Modern International Thought* (2013), Anna Becker, *Gendering the Renaissance Commonwealth* (2019), Annabel Brett, *Changes of State* (2011), C. A. Bayly, *Recovering Liberties: Indian Thought in the Age of Liberalism and Empire* (2012), Emmanuelle de Champs, *Enlightenment and Utility* (2015), Greg Conti, *Parliament the Mirror of the Nation* (2019), Katrina Forrester, *In the Shadow of Justice: Postwar Liberalism and the Remaking of Political Philosophy* (2019), Jamie Gianoutsos, *The Rule of Manhood* (2020), Eric Nelson, *The Hebrew Republic* (2010) and *The Royalist Revolution* (2014), Knud Haakonssen, *Natural Law and Moral Philosophy* (1996), Samuel Moyn, *The Last Utopia: Human Rights in History* (2010), Lucia Rubinelli, *Constituent Power* (2020), Hannah Fenichel Pitkin, *Fortune Is a Woman* (1984), Jennifer Pitts, *A Turn to Empire* (2005), Sheldon Pollock, *The Language of the Gods in the World of Men* (2016), Mira L. Seigelberg, *Statelessness: A Modern History* (2019), Michael Sonenscher, *Sans-Culottes* (2008), Richard Tuck, *Philosophy and Government 1572-1651* (1993) and *The Sleeping Sovereign* (2016).

There are now several accounts of the history of political thought from a global perspective including James Babb's *A World History of Political Thought* (2018) and Anthony Black's *A World History of*

Ancient Political Thought (2016). To combat Eurocentrism see especially Shruti Kapila and Faisai Devji, *Political Thought in Action: The Bhagavad Gita and Modern India* (2013), L. H. Liu, *The Clash of Empires: The Invention of China in Modern World Making* (2004), Watanabe Hiroshi, *A History of Japanese Political Thought, 1600–1901* (2012), Fukuzawa Yukichi and Nake Chōmin Kim Youngmin, *A History of Chinese Political Thought* (2018), Michael Cook, *Ancient Religions, Modern Politics: The Islamic Case in Comparative Perspective* (2014).

On Strauss useful guides include Stephen B. Smith's *Reading Leo Strauss: Politics, Philosophy, Judaism* (2006), his edited collection *The Cambridge Companion to Leo Strauss* (2009), and Lawrence Lampert, *The Enduring Importance of Leo Strauss* (2013). On Koselleck and *Begriffsgeschichte* see Melvin Richter's *The History of Political and Social Concepts: A Critical Introduction* (1995), Peter N. Miller, 'Nazis and Neo-Stoics: Otto Brunner and Gerhard Oestreich before and after the Second World War', *Past and Present*, 176 (2002), 144–86, and more recently Keith Tribe, 'Intellectual History as *Begriffsgeschichte*', in Richard Whatmore and Brian Young, eds, *A Companion to Intellectual History* (2015), 61–71. On Foucault see Peter Ghosh, 'Citizen or Subject? Michel Foucault in the History of Ideas', *History of European Ideas*, 24/2 (1997), 113–59, Thomas Lemke, '"The Birth of Bio-Politics": Michel Foucault's Lecture at the Collège de France on Neo-Liberal Governmentality', *Economy and Society*, 30/2 (2002), 190–207, Edward Baring, *The Young Derrida and French Philosophy, 1945–1968* (2011), François Cusset, *French Theory: How Foucault, Derrida, Deleuze, & Co. Transformed the Intellectual Life of the United States*, trans. Josephine Berganza and Marlon Jones (2008), and Michael Drolet, 'Michel Foucault and the Genealogy of Power and Knowledge', in Richard Whatmore and Brian Young, eds, *A Companion to Intellectual History* (2015), 83–96. Pocock remains the best guide to his own work: 'Present at the Creation: With Laslett to the Lost Worlds', *International Journal of Public Affairs*, 2 (2006), 7–17, 'Quentin Skinner: The History of Politics and the Politics of History', *Common Knowledge*, 10 (2004), 532–50, *Political Thought and History: Essays on Theory and Method* (Cambridge, 2009). On Quentin Skinner, James Tully's edited book *Meaning and Context: Quentin Skinner and his Critics* (1988) remains essential reading in addition to Annabel Brett and James Tully with Holly Hamilton-Bleakley, eds, *Rethinking The Foundations of Modern Political Thought* (2006). On the Cambridge School more generally see Dario Castiglione and Iain Hampsher-Monk, eds, *The History of Political Thought in National Context* (2001), Martyn P. Thomson, *Michael Oakeshott and the Cambridge School on the History of Political Thought* (2019), and Adrian Blau, 'How (Not) to Use the History of Political Thought for Contemporary Purposes', *American Journal of Political Science*, 65 (2021), 359–72.

Index

For the benefit of digital users, indexed terms that span two pages (e.g., 52–53) may, on occasion, appear on only one of those pages.

Index

THE HISTORY OF LIFE
A Very Short Introduction
Michael J. Benton

There are few stories more remarkable than the evolution of life on earth. This *Very Short Introduction* presents a succinct guide to the key episodes in that story - from the very origins of life four million years ago to the extraordinary diversity of species around the globe today. Beginning with an explanation of the controversies surrounding the birth of life itself, each following chapter tells of a major breakthrough that made new forms of life possible: including sex and multicellularity, hard skeletons, and the move to land. Along the way, we witness the greatest mass extinction, the first forests, the rise of modern ecosystems, and, most recently, conscious humans.

www.oup.com/vsi

ONLINE CATALOGUE
A Very Short Introduction

Our online catalogue is designed to make it easy to find your ideal Very Short Introduction. View the entire collection by subject area, watch author videos, read sample chapters, and download reading guides.

http://fds.oup.com/www.oup.co.uk/general/vsi/index.html

SOCIAL MEDIA
Very Short Introduction

Join our community
www.oup.com/vsi

- Join us online at the official Very Short Introductions **Facebook** page.
- Access the thoughts and musings of our authors with our online **blog**.
- Sign up for our monthly **e-newsletter** to receive information on all new titles publishing that month.
- Browse the full range of Very Short Introductions online.
- Read **extracts** from the Introductions for free.
- Visit our library of **Reading Guides**. These guides, written by our expert authors will help you to question again, why you think what you think.
- If you are a teacher or lecturer you can order inspection copies quickly and simply via our website.